The Ghosts of Walter Crockett

A Memoir

Also from Islandport Press

Take it Easy: Portland in the 1970s
By John Duncan

Whatever It Takes
By May Davidson

Shoutin' into the Fog
By Thomas Hanna

Hauling by Hand
By Dean Lawrence Lunt

Available at www.islandportpress.com

The Ghosts of Walter Crockett

A Memoir

By W. Edward Crockett

ISLANDPORT PRESS

ISLANDPORT PRESS

Islandport Press
P.O. Box 10
Yarmouth, Maine 04096
www.islandportpress.com
info@islandportpress.com

All Photographs, unless otherwise noted,
courtesy of W. Edward Crockett.
First Edition Printed November 2021

ISBN: 978-1-952143-21-2
Library of Congress Control Number: 2021935311

Dean L. Lunt, Editor-in-Chief | Publisher
Dylan Andrews, Book Designer

*Opposite (left to right): Ted, Seth, Mattie, Scott, Martha, and me.
Back cover (clockwise from top left): Jimmy, David, Gin, Marie,
Danny, Me, Walt, and Carolyn.*

For Seth, Mattie, and Ted,

May My Life's Lessons Serve You Well

Love, Dad

Table of Contents

Introduction

The first line of his obituary in the *Portland Press Herald* proclaimed my father, Walter Crockett, "the biggest drunk in Portland."

It was right there in black and white. Of course, I didn't need to see it in print to know the truth. I lived it. It haunted me my whole life. *The Ghosts of Walter Crockett* tells his story from my perspective as I tried to understand and deal with it all.

I am a Portland kid born and bred, having lived here for all but five years of my life. I grew up in the 1960s and 1970s on Munjoy Hill in a modest two-family house on Kellogg Street with my mother, seven siblings, and numerous stray cats and dogs. My maternal grandparents, Howard and Nellie Mayberry, resided in the apartment upstairs. Grampa was a laborer with a binge drinking problem, while Grammy, like my mom, was a homemaker. Not surprisingly the family didn't have much money, by which I really mean we didn't have any money. My father left our home when I was two years old and spent my entire youth on the streets of Portland, its most identifiable skid row bum. We became "products of the State," surviving thanks to its support.

My maternal grandparents arrived in Portland via Boston during the Great Depression with their two daughters, Ginny (my mom) and Millie. Grammy's roots (Feeneys and Hannigans) were in Sligo, Ireland, and Grampa's clan hailed from Glasgow, Scotland. Grammy was a cousin of the great film director John Feeney, who changed his name to John Ford. I never knew my paternal grandparents. Harrison Crockett died long before I was born, and Delia Clancy Crockett passed away shortly thereafter. My father had eight brothers and one sister. Seven of his siblings, like him, struggled with alcohol addiction.

My parents met in 1957 and married a year later. My mom had five kids from a previous marriage, then three more with my father. I am the baby of the family. I didn't really appreciate that moniker as a child, but I totally endorse it now. For about five years we were all a big happy family, until the shit hit the fan and Walter checked out. The metaphorical and literal heart of my young world spanned from Munjoy Hill to Monument Square. Since my mother never learned to drive, I walked or took public transportation everywhere. My home, schools, church, and even my first four jobs were within this physical footprint. Coincidentally, it was my father's domain as well. I loved growing up on the Hill and am proud of my neighborhood, of the very real people who lived and labored there, mostly Irish, Italian, and Jewish immigrant families. The Hill is imprinted in my DNA.

Back then, Portland was a careworn, working-class city. There was no Arts District, no tourists paying a grand a night to stay in a boutique hotel, and no one was dropping a million dollars for a waterfront condo. It had a lot of history. Following the Great Fire of 1866, Portland rebuilt itself into a modern, prosperous city and it stayed that way through the early 1900s. But the Great Depression, followed by World War II, did a number on the fortunes of Portland—new investment stopped, the economy shifted, and the vibrancy of downtown moved to the ascendant suburbs. Everything just seemed to get old. By the 1960s, the waterfront, an area that is now part of the trendy Old Port, was derelict and dangerous. Congress Street, the once-booming retail district, was cracking. The State Theater turned to pornography to save itself from the wrecking ball and it was easy to find a dive bar or an all-night club or drugs or a lady of the night. Yet, the most scandalous changes to the face of the city were caused by urban renewal. Urban planners of the era thought that more roads and parking spaces were the golden ticket. In Portland, entire blocks and neighborhoods were razed following the stroke of a pen. Near my home, Franklin Street sprouted into the four-lane Franklin Arterial. To make way for the wider road, more than one hundred houses were demolished and hundreds of people were relocated. Other city streets were rerouted or bulldozed to accommodate better traffic flow, damn the folks that lived there. The new Franklin Arterial effectively severed the Munjoy Hill neighborhood from the city's downtown, deepening our sense of isolation and heightening our inferiority complex. We already had a chip on our shoulder, and it only got bigger when city planners made it official—Munjoy Hill was on the wrong side of the tracks.

All of this served as the backdrop to my daily life and looming over it all was my father. You see, my father spent most of his time straddling the arterial himself. His most frequent hangouts were Kennedy Park, the Cathedral Block, Lincoln Park and the jail that sat right on it, while Portland's only flophouse, the 24-Hour Club on India Street, the Old Port, and Monument Square were just blocks away. I could not escape him.

When he wasn't in my face, he was a spirit lurking in the shadows. Sometimes I felt his presence, other times I shivered; his predicament plagued me. My father was always drunk on the downtown streets—often sleeping on a bench in Lincoln Park, sometimes curled up against a building near the waterfront, or sprawled out in a local jail cell sobering up, if he was lucky.

When I was fourteen and attending Cheverus High School, I would wait for the school bus at the edge of Lincoln Park. On too many mornings, I would spy him out of the corner of my eye, a deeply flawed and crumbled mess of a man passed out on a bench reeking of alcohol. My friends sometimes nudged me and said, "Hey, isn't that your dad?"

I wouldn't answer; I would just turn away. That time spent waiting for the school bus, no matter how fleeting in reality, was simply soul-crushing. In those moments, I hated him.

But the human soul is an amazing thing. No matter how hard I tried, no matter how aloof I pretended to be, and no matter how much I cried, I could never shake the fact that the ghost who haunted my dreams, and would do so by hook or by crook for the rest of my life, was my father. That meant something whether I wanted it to or not. Our lives would be entwined whether I lived in Portland, Orono, or Houston, Texas. I tried to pretend he didn't exist or that he was just another faceless bum. I thought I could, but I couldn't. Compassion and forgiveness are critical parts of humanity. I couldn't escape his shadow. I couldn't forget that he was my father no matter how many mistakes he made. I knew that his brothers all fell victim to the bottle in one way or another. That their blood was my blood. No, that he was my father was a simple undeniable, biological fact. Still, the question that troubled me for years was this: "Am I destined to be just like him?"

It probably didn't help my psyche that my mother would admonish me by saying, "If you drink, you will end up just like your father: on the street."

As a result, the young boy crushed by the sight of his drunken dad on a park bench desperately wanted to race as far away as he could, thinking if he ran far enough, he wouldn't be embarrassed by him; wouldn't become a bum like him. But the path forward for the man I became was fraught with mental demons rooted in my father and my own dances with alcohol. Researching and writing this book has been a fascinating and, at times, therapeutic journey. And as I finished, it was once again right there in front of me in black and white—the biggest drunk in Portland was my dad. Reconciling that mentally, trying to rise from poverty to find success and happiness, being a good father to my kids, understanding the power of forgiveness, and living my best life, has proven to be my lifelong quest. And hard as it may have been to imagine, I couldn't have done it without him.

My father in his Army days. He was still a teenager in this picture.

Chapter One
Walter Crockett

M y father, Walter Crockett, was born March 28, 1933, in
Portland, to Harrison Crockett and Delia Clancy Crockett.
He grew up on Munjoy Hill and was one of ten children: Harrison
"Lolly," William "Brud," Francis, John "Duddy," Robert, Margaret
"Sister," Carroll, Eugene, Walter, and Phillip.

For most of his youth, the Crockett clan moved from apartment to apartment, sometimes by choice, but often because they
were evicted after not paying the rent. They lived mostly around
Portland's East Bayside neighborhood. In the 1930s and 1940s,
East Bayside was populated with working-class people and lots of
Irish folk, but much of the area, including a few apartment buildings once occupied by the Crocketts, was razed in the 1960s. New
construction began on Kennedy Park in 1964, when 160 public
housing rental units were built for poor and low-income residents.
In 1967, everything from Back Cove to Casco Bay was blown to
smithereens when construction on the Franklin Arterial began;
more than one hundred structures were leveled, forcing hundreds
of people to relocate. In 1969, Portland's tallest residential edifice,
Franklin Towers, was erected on the corner of Cumberland Avenue
and Wilmot Street. Overall, between the demolitions authorized by

Portland's Slum Clearance and Redevelopment Administration in the late 1950s and urban renewal in the 1960s, the neighborhoods along what is now Franklin Arterial from Back Cove to Commercial Street were radically changed.

By all accounts, my father, Walter Crockett, as a young teenager was a bright and talented young man, but it is also universally acknowledged that he lacked motivation and direction. And he had already developed a debilitating taste for alcohol. By day he helped his seven older brothers at their jobs, and by night he joined them again as what was known as a "Dump Ranger," people who raided the dump, primarily for wood. He was an athletic kid who played football and baseball and loved the Boston Red Sox, but boxing was his favorite sport. My Uncle William "Brud" Crockett, my namesake and one of Walter's older brothers, told me, "He liked boxing a little too much; he wouldn't back down from a fight which often proved troublesome."

Back then what he enjoyed perhaps even more than fighting and alcohol, was belting out tunes, particularly Irish songs. He was blessed with powerful pipes and a nice deep brogue. He was a valued member of the church choir.

In 1948, after Walter graduated from eighth grade at Cathedral Junior High, he dropped out of school for good. That summer he was fifteen and he hitchhiked to New York City with his buddy, Jeep. His goal was to hang out in the Bowery district of Manhattan and drink. He wore a beat-up, discolored sweatshirt that clashed with his corduroy pants and Boston Red Sox cap. Those were his only clothes. He and Jeep set off on an adventure with no plans in mind other than getting drunk and roaming the city. He probably should have left the Red Sox cap at home.

Walter had heard about the Bowery from his older brothers and their stories were alluring to the teenager. He couldn't wait to get there to hang with the local winos and bums.

The Bowery, which was tucked into lower Manhattan, was in disarray with a lot of run-down tenement houses and abandoned buildings. At all hours, drunken men sat on the stoops, drinking conspicuously out of brown paper bags and moving only to stagger down a nearby alley to relieve themselves. The local authorities were aware of the hubbub in the Bowery. The country was still rebounding from World War II and unfortunately many of the bums hanging out there were former servicemen who fought for freedom, but were down on their luck. New York's finest chose not to rain on their parade. Walter, cocky as hell, and Jeep waltzed right in. Here they were, not of legal age to drink, vote, or enlist, swigging whiskey and cheap wine as fast as they could get their hands on it.

On some nights, Walter even entertained his new friends with Irish tributes like "When Irish Eyes Are Smiling."

When Irish eyes are smiling,
sure 'tis like a morn in spring.
In the lilt of Irish laughter
you can hear the angels sing.

At the end of each concert he would boast, "The next time you'll hear me, it'll be on Broadway." His proclamation never came true. Finally one night, Walter got into an argument with a drunken Yankees fan.

The Yankees fan called Red Sox shortstop Johnny Pesky a dipshit and Walter jumped all over him. "What's your fuckin' problem? Watch your mouth before I shut it."

"You and what fuckin' army? Look around, asshole, a lot more Yankees fans around here. You should be embarrassed to wear that piece of shit hat."

Walter resorted to what he knew best; he knocked the Yankees fan on his ass with a right cross. But while turning to celebrate his punch, he was blindsided by a whiskey bottle behind his right ear. It would not be his last battle scar.

Two days later, out of money and luck, the boys hitchhiked back home.

In Portland, Walter lived with his mother and some of his siblings on Cleeve Street at the foot of Munjoy Hill. Most days Walter slept in, but occasionally he'd rise early and toil alongside one of his brothers to make a few bucks. Then he'd pound some beers and mostly find trouble the rest of the day and night.

At fifteen, Walter was already a regular in the Portland bars. He even had his own cuff, or charge account, in many. Although Walter enjoyed getting shit-faced, he didn't like waking up feeling sluggish and shitty. So rather than stop drinking, he advanced to hard liquor and only drank beer when nothing else was available. This routine quickly grew old with his mom (his father passed away when he was a toddler). Even his brothers, who were well on their way to becoming alcoholics themselves, tired of their little bro mooching on their earnings to drink.

My Uncle Brud, a successful local bookie, was generous to his younger siblings, often giving them drinking money. Not surprisingly, Uncle Brud was my father's favorite brother. He was a clever guy and very cunning, and, like Walter, he dropped out of school at fifteen. But unlike my father, Uncle Brud maintained steady jobs, first as a busboy in a local restaurant and then driving an Old

Tavern Farm milk truck. It was Brud who stepped up to support the family financially after their father passed away.

By the time Walter reached seventeen, Brud began advising him to get on with his life and start doing something. Unfortunately, my father's options were limited. Going to college was out of the question since he hadn't set foot in a classroom since eighth grade, and becoming a bookie, although risky and illegal, was already covered by his siblings. He did have a good left hook and racked up a pretty impressive amateur boxing record at the local rec center, but he wasn't good enough to make a living.

Given the limited options in Portland, Uncle Brud encouraged Walter to join the U.S. Army. Brud served in the Army during World War II, and believed it might be Walter's only chance to escape his obvious downward spiral.

So, on a fall morning in 1950, Walter, only a few months shy of his eighteenth birthday, slumped onto Brud's milk truck to begin what he assumed was another routine day. Hungover from the previous night's carousing, he quickly fell asleep in the truck. He was useless, which once again pissed off his brother. Brud decided to cut deliveries short and drove straight to the closest recruiting station. He parked and yelled at his younger brother.

"Walta, you piece of shit, wake up! It is time you got off your ass and did something."

A startled Walter shot up.

"For Christ's sake, what the fuck's your problem?

Brud pointed at the Army Recruiting Office and said, "We're going in."

My father thought the world of Uncle Brud. He trusted him and sometimes actually listened to him. I think he knew his current path was a poor one, and things needed to change. But the Army? He also knew that since he was still only 17 his mother had to sign him over to the Army. That could be his ticket to not joining. Turns out that wasn't a problem. Uncle Brud had already discussed his plan with her and she was on board.

She told Uncle Brud, "For Walter, it's go in the Army, or go to jail." She had already signed papers so he could enlist.

And so, Walter Crockett joined the U.S. Army.

In 1950, America was just getting involved in the Korean War and the fact that a war was in progress actually appealed to Walter. He loved his country and was proud of all the men who served before him, especially his brothers and all the veterans he met out on the streets. He figured he was destined for the infantry, and that was fine with him. He was bused to Fort Dix, an Army base located southeast of Trenton, New Jersey, for basic training. He was immediately assigned to the 39th Infantry Regiment.

After ten weeks of boot camp, he came home for a visit. While drinking beers on a stoop he declared to a few buddies, "Once I'm back to boot camp, I'm thinking about going to jump school."

They mocked him. "You'll never make it."

In other words, his friends didn't think he had what it took to jump from airplanes as a paratrooper. Predictably, that was just the push Walter needed. When he returned to camp, he immediately volunteered for jump school. When he finished basic training, he was bused to Fort Benning to become a paratrooper. Fort Benning straddles the Alabama-Georgia state line and it was there that the U.S. Army Ranger School was formed to create a special breed of fighting men, the Army Rangers. The intent was to develop combat skills for select soldiers and craft a realistic tactical environment. The U.S. Army Airborne School, or Jump School, was also at Fort Benning.

Walter had never even been on an airplane before joining the Army. He joked: "I made dozens of jumps before actually landing in a plane."

But he was a hustler and a risk taker. Not that becoming a select paratrooper wasn't incentive enough, but the realization that he could make an additional fifty dollars per month jumping out of airplanes enticed him even more. It proved to be a bold choice; he was destined for the 82nd Airborne Division, one that specialized in parachute assault operations all over the world. It was highly mobile. In World War II, the 82nd was part of the Normandy invasion and the Battle of the Bulge.

Life in the 82nd in the 1950s demanded rigorous exercise in all environments at numerous locations throughout the continental United States. In addition to long runs and strength conditioning, there were glider drills, instruction in parachute making, and paratrooper best practices to master.

He was becoming a good soldier, yet probably didn't realize how his decision to become a paratrooper most likely saved his life. After jump school, Walter and his 82nd Airborne comrades were moved to Fort Bragg in North Carolina. By 1950, Fort Bragg had more than forty thousand men on its grounds, including the Green Berets.

Due to the Cold War, Walter and the 82nd Airborne were on guard and gearing up for possible conflict with Russia. The United States wanted the regiment ready in case Russia mounted a ground assault anywhere in the world. As a result, it was never deployed to action in Korea. Meanwhile, many of his mates from basic training were deployed and killed in action.

When not training, Walter relaxed by hitting the local clubs. Before going into the Army he had to scrape up money or use cuffs to buy drinks, but in the service finding drinks was easy. Not surprisingly he got into a few scuffles here and there; after all, he still thought of himself as a pugilist and now he had been trained by the Army.

After his discharge, Walter returned home to Portland. He served his time, but had no interest in making the Army a career. Unfortunately, not much had changed in his hometown and finding work proved challenging. Army service didn't change his status as a high-school dropout and jumping out of airplanes wasn't a relevant skill for work in the Port City. He hadn't really changed much in the way of ambition or dependability, either. The only jobs he found, and then only sporadically, were as a handyman or laborer. When he did work, many considered him, "arguably the best bricklayer around," but you couldn't count on him.

My father (right) and two of his Army buddies pose with bottles of rum and whiskey in the 1950s.

At this point, he was 22, had no high school education, and no real job, but he was already an alcoholic. Over the next few years, he wandered about the Portland Waterfront, went on drinking binges, got arrested, and failed to regularly show up for work. When he got arrested, he'd usually get locked up for thirty days at the Cumberland County Jail. The only upside of those arrests? They gave him a place to live and forced him to get sober, even if only in short stretches.

My mom as a young woman.

Chapter Two
Virginia Mayberry

Virginia "Ginny" Mayberry was born on Feb. 17, 1923, the daughter of Howard S. and Ellen "Nellie" (Hannigan) Mayberry. Ginny was born in Roxbury, Massachusetts, and moved to Portland with her parents and younger sister, Millie, as a child. Her father worked as a truck driver and her mother was a cleaning lady at the offices around Monument Square. She attended only parochial schools, graduating from Cathedral High School in 1941. As a senior in high school, Ginny seriously considered entering the convent. Thankfully, she had a change of heart.

In 1944, when she was 21, she married David Paul, a veteran. The young couple had five children starting in 1945: David, Marie, Jimmy, Gin, and Danny. Danny was born in 1953. Her marriage to David failed due to his infidelity. After learning that he had had a child by another woman, Ginny, a feisty, old-fashioned Irish Catholic, decided she could no longer excuse his transgressions. He left quietly, returning to his native Kentucky, and was never heard from again, save for a small monthly check that arrived in the mail. My five older siblings didn't really know their father. The two oldest kept in touch, but the three youngest chose to have nothing to do with him.

By the late 1950s, my mother was a divorcée who lived in an apartment on Kellogg Street in Munjoy Hill. She lived with her five kids, ages three to twelve, and shared a two-story, two-unit home with her parents. Ginny and the kids lived on the first floor, while her parents lived upstairs. She worked as a waitress downtown to help pay the bills.

In the fall of 1957, Ginny met my father. One of Walter's Army pals was dating a friend of hers and lined up a double date. She was ten years his senior. Honestly, although obviously I'm relieved that they did stay together, it's somewhat surprising my parents had a second date. My father's first encounter with the entire Paul clan must have been daunting. When he arrived to pick up Ginny, all five of her kids peered out the window to check him out. He also suspected that her parents were lurking somewhere behind the flowing drapes that adorned the windows. It must have been an intimidating introduction.

My mom was attracted to Walter's big blue eyes, and the fact that he was ten years younger than her. My dad was immediately attracted to her feistiness and competitiveness. For their date, they went to the candlepin bowling lanes on Forest Avenue. Rumor has it that Ginny was an excellent bowler and kicked Walter's ass, forever endearing herself to him.

No question, Ginny lacked confidence and good judgment when it came to men. Walter was good-looking, charming, and nice to her kids (at least when he was sober). The courtship period ended and nuptials happened quickly when Ginny found out she was pregnant in the summer of 1958. Being a churchgoing, devout Catholic girl, having a child out of wedlock was not an option. Walter, brought up a good Catholic himself, understood and agreed. They were soon wed, although not in the Catholic church since a church wedding was prohibited for a divorcee at the time. They had three children, Walter, Carolyn, and myself, in a span of two and a half years. I was born in 1961. It got off to a good start, but it went south quickly. Eight children—three of his own on top of Ginny's five—proved disastrous for Walter, who could barely support himself, let alone a family of ten.

By the time I was born, a typical day for Walter, especially in the summer, went something like this: After sleeping in to nurse his ever-present hangover, he'd scrounge up whatever bits of food he could find, grab a fresh beer, plant his ass on his slip-covered, broken-down recliner, and listen to Boston Red Sox games on the radio. Meanwhile, Ginny ran around like a chicken with its head cut off tending to the eight kids. Their living room was sparsely furnished. It included a sofa, which was mainly used by the cats to sharpen their claws, a recliner, and a folding card table. If the Sox were losing or if he'd already downed too many beers, any kids within earshot would get an earful from my father.

"Jesus Christ, Jimmy, cut the shit. Go outside if you can't keep it down."

Jimmy was one of his stepchildren.

"Watch your mouth. This is our house, we don't have to listen to you."

"You little shit. If ya know what's good for ya you'll get your ass outside!"

Of course the bickering escalated into a full-blown fight when Ginny intervened. Then, Walter would storm out of the house to trade his recliner for a barstool.

In short, a guy who lacked motivation and ran away from even the smallest responsibility by seeking solace with a bottle, was now expected to provide for eight children despite lacking a complete

My mom, possibly on her wedding day.

education or any real skills. Walter also lacked what mattered most—accountability and mental toughness. He was strong physically, but crumbled when confronted with adversity or responsibility. He held up okay for a year or so, but following the birth of his third and final child (me), he simply fell apart. He would go missing for weeks, sometimes even months. During the two years following my birth, Walter repeatedly went on drinking binges. He was out of control; and as a result he couldn't hold onto a job. Ginny later discovered that he wasn't always "missing"—sometimes he was locked up in the local jail for thirty days on charges of public drunkenness. No one bothered to tell her.

Regardless of the reasons, Walter simply was not around and was not helping his family. The Paul-Crockett clan had each other, and not much else. Ginny was developing a variety of health problems, including high blood pressure, high cholesterol, heart issues, and depression. She was only about 40 when doctors advised her to stop working. Before her health began to wane, Ginny worked as a waitress at The Blaine Restaurant. Now, when the family desperately needed support, Walter wasn't contributing financially.

His occasional visits to the house in the early 1960s, usually went something like this:

Walter would come stumbling down the street, drunk and ornery, and pound on the front door. Ginny would secure the kids in their rooms, race out to the door, and pull him inside before the whole neighborhood got wind of it.

"Ssshhh, I just put the babies down."

Then, looking at him in disgust, "For cryin' out loud, where have you been?"

"Aahh, where do you think I've been," he says, holding up his brown paper bag. "I can't get any peace and quiet here with all these goddamn kids."

"And another thing, why don't you turn on some fuckin' heat in this place. It's freezing!"

"Listen, asshole, we need money to buy heat and since you haven't worked in months, this is as warm as it gets. Maybe you should get off your ass and find some work so that your children don't freeze to death."

At this point Walter would usually brush by, give her the one-finger salute, and crash on the recliner.

By law as long as Walter called 60 Kellogg Street home, Ginny did not qualify for welfare services. The family was dead broke, so it finally came time for hard decisions.

That time was the fall of 1963. I was two years old. My mother met my father on the front porch of the apartment on Kellogg Street and told him flat out that he couldn't live at home anymore.

My father holding Walt on the steps of a local house.

Five years into marriage, an institution she unequivocally believed in, she was forced to choose between her husband and her children. When it's said that way, it sounds like an easy choice, but it's never that simple.

Ginny was a devout Catholic, and from her perspective, she had already disgraced herself once with a divorce. She didn't want to travel down that road again, but something in this relationship had to give. When Walter was sober he at least contributed something toward the health and welfare of the family, but those moments were increasingly rare. Ginny leaned on her parents to stay afloat. As Walter spiraled deeper into his personal abyss, the need to feed and clothe her children finally forced her to kick him out.

Making it even tougher was that in 1963 most women like my mother didn't quit. They were expected to hang in there even with a deeply flawed man, for better or worse.

There were problems all around us. Our neighborhood had a lot of "bad" going on—poverty, alcohol abuse, drug dealing, physical abuse, mental abuse, pedophilia, and even incest.

In our home, the root issues were primarily poverty and alcohol. We didn't have a "pot to piss in." We were dirt poor, white trash, and seemingly destined to make the same mistakes as our extended family, our friends, and our neighbors. Mom was broke, raising eight children, and dealing with growing health issues that left her essentially unemployable. Despite all this, remarkably, the Catholic Church and even some friends and neighbors tabbed *her* as the bad person in this situation.

The cold hard truth was this: If Walter, an alcoholic who didn't work, lived at home, the family did not qualify for state support, such as food stamps, other welfare funding, and health care.

Kicking him out was her only option. Her decision, perhaps more than any other, gave me and my siblings the chance at a better life.

My mother is my hero. I think about her every day.

When the deal was done, as it turns out, Walter didn't put up much of a fight. He disappeared that same day. He briefly stayed with his sister Peggy at her apartment in Kennedy Park, and then spent the next seventeen years living on the streets. Walter became *the* town drunk and a public embarrassment to his family.

That left my mother, Virginia Mayberry Crockett, to raise eight children, including three preschoolers, in 1960s Portland. Despite everything that swirled around her and the challenges we faced, my mother steadfastly believed that a child could prevail over the "bad" with help and support. She brushed aside her ego and counted on common sense. She leaned on her parents, who were invaluable. We couldn't have survived without them.

I believed in my mother. She was eccentric and flawed, but her faith in God, which was espoused before her children ad nauseam, was unflappable. Although her ways were at times unorthodox, she remains the wisest person I've ever known. She was unhappy with her predicament, but she would be damned if life wasn't going to be different for her children no matter the odds.

"You can be better than this," she would constantly tell me.

Even though her husbands were deeply flawed, her health poor, and her self-esteem worn, she never lost faith. And since faith was her foundation, it was no surprise that Ma, as we called her, became our rock.

Chapter Three
The Hill

I lived in that two-story, two-family house on the corner of Kellogg and Monument streets in Portland's Munjoy Hill neighborhood for the first twenty-one years of my life. My grandparents lived in the upstairs apartment with some of the older kids, while Ma and her younger children settled on the first floor.

I'll be straight: Yes, it was my home, but it was a wretched house.

Our tiny front yard was protected by an antique black wrought-iron fence that gave the house an Addams Family aura. The house itself was odd-looking. It was shaped like a box and had a mansard roof with slate shingles accenting the second level and decorative window moldings throughout. Guests and residents entered through weather-beaten Victorian pocket doors then proceeded through a set of rugged Brownstone doors into a wide foyer with high clapboard walls and a raised ceiling leading to a winding staircase and the second story.

Once through the front doors, the hall separated the main level into two parts with a point of entry on each side. Past the door to the left were two bedrooms (you had to walk through the first to get to the second. One of them was mine). Across the hall on the

My grandparents, Howard S. and Ellen "Nellie" Mayberry, in the 1920s.

right was the rest of the apartment. You entered through the living room, which was centered on this side of the house, between
Ma's makeshift bedroom to the front and the kitchen area, which
included a small pantry and an adjacent bathroom, in the back. The
toilet was the only private space in this part of the house since none
of the other rooms had doors.

Kellogg Street is a short street consisting of two blocks running
from Congress to Adams streets, dumping into Munjoy South.
Sometime in the '60s, the triple-decker beside us on the corner
of Monument Street was torn down. Just watching the structure
come down was cool, but as an added bonus, its demolition created
more parking and play space. It also gave Grammy a glimpse of
Casco Bay from her upstairs bedroom window. Sixty years later that
glimpse would be marketed as an ocean view and a selling point for
local realtor esate agents.

At its most crowded, the first-floor apartment contained my
mother, six of her kids, thirteen cats, and three dogs.

I suppose 60 Kellogg Street had some charm, but it was a
calamity. Thankfully, the city health inspector wasn't aware of its
condition. There's no way it would have passed an inspection.

The sixteen animals were all strays that became house pets
because Ma couldn't bear to set them loose. And often, it seemed
humans were actually behind them on the food chain. It was maddening enough that the pets shed everywhere, but since Ma didn't
have the energy or desire to keep tabs on them, we were expected
to walk the dogs and change the litter boxes. I always gave her a
hard time about the animals, and repeatedly blew off her requests
for help. As a result when the dogs had "to go," they found a spot in
the house "to go." There was piss and shit and fur balls everywhere,
sometimes going undisturbed for days. When I actually did try to
pick up the dog or cat shit, I sometimes would gag and actually

vomit, only adding to the grossness. The stench at times, especially on hot summer days, was overwhelming.

Our furniture was in shambles; crumpled, clawed, and covered with cat hair. In addition, one of my brothers was a bed-wetter into his early teens. We did not have a washing machine so his bedding sat for days before being noticed and changed. I slept in that room for most of my childhood, and it reeked. I laugh now, but back then I was distraught. The stench from it all was nearly unbearable. I knew it was unsanitary, but I couldn't do much about it.

Out of frustration and anger I occasionally screamed, "Thanks, Dad!"

Even as a kid, I knew the place was a dump and I eventually stopped inviting friends over to my house. I was embarrassed; it was disgusting. My brother David would say, "We know who our real friends are; they're the ones that keep coming back."

I had one close friend who rang the doorbell regularly, but never came into the house. Ever. We never talked about it and didn't have to. I understood.

Obviously, keeping a clean house was not my mother's calling. Early in my life, my older sisters Marie and Gin helped right the ship to some degree, but once they moved out the place simply went to hell. Ma was tired; her spirit was shot, and she was obviously depressed. At the end of the day I guess living in a clean house just wasn't important to her. I know people thought less of her, and by extension less of us, because of the home she kept. I grudgingly accepted that this was the case, opting to give her a pass and just surmising others were missing the bigger picture.

Ma always had a saying that I took to heart: "Do as I say, not as I do." She recognized her shortcomings and hoped her children would see beyond them. Although some interpreted her wisdom as excuses, I preferred to focus on the intent.

My family was not unique in having problems.

In the 1960s and '70s, Kellogg Street itself was a troubled spot. Just beyond our iron gate were run-down tenement buildings and public housing units leading to the Munjoy South complex, basic row housing for low-income families, at the foot of Kellogg Street. Many of the homes, like ours, were dealing with some heavy and difficult issues.

The blocks surrounding our house became our playing fields since nobody wanted to stay inside. Munjoy South had a playground with a basketball court and an open area for throwing and kicking all varieties of balls. I spent many sunny days in and around Munjoy South playing sports. If I wasn't shooting hoops, I was playing stickball or running around the playground. Although relatively small, the playground was nice and had all the usual apparatuses, swings, a slide, a sandbox and a merry-go-round. If not hanging out in Munjoy South, I was usually in the neighborhood playing football, hitting a tennis ball, or playing Wiffle ball.

Although ten homes lined Kellogg Street between Congress and Monument there were rarely any cars parked on the street. Many families, like ours, didn't own a vehicle. And if they did, it was only one, and it was parked in the single-lane driveway next to the house. We (all the neighborhood kids and anyone else who showed up) would play touch football all day, right on the street. The telephone pole at Monument Street was one end zone, and the big oak tree in front of Mrs. Richio's house was the other. It was just us kids, no adults, and we picked teams and officiated games ourselves. There weren't many arguments or fights, unless I got pouty.

As a kid, sports were everything and all I really had. I would smack a tennis ball against the brick foundation of the apartment building at the corner of Kellogg and Congress for hours. The structure was built into the hill so at the top (along Congress

Street) the brick foundation was about one foot high before the siding began. At the opposite end the brick was about five feet high. I hit balls there for years before I ever played tennis on a real court. My siblings and I were competitive. We'd keep score at everything. I was the youngest and usually smallest, and although I secured my share of wins, I was never the *best* at anything until we hit the tennis court. I never lost a tennis match within the family and was proud of it. Silly, I know, but that brick wall brought me solace and confidence.

I wasn't much of a baseball player, but I loved Wiffle ball. Our diamond was the T-intersection at Waterville and Monument streets. The bases were compliments of the city. First base was the stop sign at the corner; second base was the fire hydrant at the top of the intersection in front of the Poolers' house; third base was the street sign on the other corner. Home plate was painted in the middle of Waterville Street. Occasionally we'd play a real game, which meant running the bases, but most of the time the type of hits were automatics or we played home run derby. We set up teams and leagues, and kept records and awarded home run and batting titles; it was a blast. We played from sunup to sundown. It kept us out of trouble, which I guess was the whole idea.

It was no secret that drugs were rampant, gangs were prevalent, and the most troublesome hangout on Munjoy Hill, The Corner, was only a few blocks from our Wiffle ball field. Many of my childhood friends got sucked into life at The Corner, and the consequences were always damaging. I was also lucky to have an adult role model who played Wiffle ball with us, Dale Rand.

Dale's brother-in-law, Mike, was my age and one of the Wiffle ball regulars. Dale had young children of his own. Yet most every weekend Dale would play with the neighborhood kids—Wiffle ball in the summer and tackle football on the Eastern Promenade in the winter. Dale wasn't there to organize the activities, but to show us how to play the right way and have fun.

I didn't have a father at home, but yearned for a father-like figure. I often said, "When I become a father I want to be like Dale Rand." He was there for all the kids, not just his own. He embodied what a father, brother, and son should be. He was kind yet firm, silly, yet deep. Most notably he cared about us. We needed guidance because The Hill was an easy place to find trouble.

Daily life at home, other than at Christmastime, was mundane. If I wasn't at school or church, I was outside playing (I have already mentioned the condition of our house). The routine only varied come the holiday season when Ma stepped it up for Christmas. We'd get the tree early and keep it up until January 6 since that's when she said the three wise men arrived at the manger in Bethlehem. We'd hang our stockings—Ma's, eight kids, favored felines, and eventually grandkids—around the double-wide door sill in the living room. We decorated the tree and placed drawings in the windows.

My favorite decorations were the plastic four-foot-tall Noel candles that we put on top of the front porch roof. To secure them, I'd get buckets of sand from the sandbox at Sheridan Street (sort of a gift from the city) and lug them back home to fill the two candles so that they wouldn't fall over. I'd climb out an upstairs window onto the roof and align them perfectly. I don't recall seeing Noel candles anywhere else; I'm sure that's why I liked them so much. Christmastime was festive and temporarily concealed an otherwise dreary existence.

Although I didn't realize it when I was young, subconsciously I was angry at my father. I asked questions like, "Where is Dad? How come he's never around?" Ma and the older siblings deflected

This picture shows some of the more than a dozen cats and three dogs that lived in our house. That's my brother Walt, the center of their attention, in the living room.

such inquiries, and I didn't really dwell on his absence. I was young and couldn't remember him living with us anyway, so moving felt painless, but it clearly wasn't. Even though I had four older brothers, and a grandfather who lived upstairs, I didn't view them as role models straightaway. Walt was too young, and the other three were preoccupied with plotting their way off Kellogg Street. That left me, justifiably so, mostly as an afterthought.

My suppressed anger often surfaced in a quick-trigger temper, and it usually flashed in competition. I liked to win, still do, but I was a poor sport. Growing up the baby in the family I was usually the youngest and smallest kid playing. I'd storm off, or worse, start crying, if I lost a touch football or hoops game. I'm sure once or twice I took my ball and went home, ending everybody's good time. I was fifteen before I finally got a handle on my emotions and stopped being a crybaby.

My maternal grandparents, especially my grandmother supported my mother unconditionally, and they are the reason we had a roof over our heads.

Nellie, or Grammy as I called her, was the matriarch of our clan.

Shrewdly, Ginny leaned on Nellie at every turn, from dealing with Walter, to running the household, to raising the kids, to helping guide our escape routes out of Dodge. She persevered amid related perils and was always present for us. She was the most resilient human I've ever known. So spirited and encouraging, she gave us protection and a will to succeed.

She was my first financial advisor. I never had a bank account until I was an adult. Didn't need one. Grammy locked my savings in a small gray metal box in her chest of drawers. Siblings would ask me, "Why don't you open a bank account and collect interest?"

I'd laugh and say, "No way, running upstairs is handier and the interest is much better."

She spoiled me.

As for my grandfather, I loved him, but I was afraid of him.

Howard Mayberry was intimidating. It wasn't his size per se, he was about five-foot, ten-inches tall and probably one hundred and eighty pounds, but it was his Bunyanesque presence that scared me. Grampa was an alcoholic, like my father, but by the mid-1960s he was clean. When he was younger, he was a classic binge drinker who'd go missing for days, then bounce back and stay sober for months. He beat it when I was a toddler, and I have no recollection of him drinking. Grampa seldom spoke, but he could burn a hole through me with his menacing stare. He had a soft spot for my father; clearly they had alcohol in common, and he accepted Walter's fate. I figured out later that he was a softie, a real teddy bear, but he never let on. He died my senior year of high school, and I regret not tapping into his genius. He was a sage; I suspect that's where much of my mother's wisdom originated. We've all heard the saying, "Youth is wasted on the young." When I think about Grampa, I consider that axiom. I lamented not having a father, which was stupid since I had Grampa upstairs.

Some of my fondest memories were sitting between my grandparents at their kitchen table while they played whist against Uncle John, Grammy's brother, and his friend Rose. I'd listen to their banter for hours on end and study Grampa as he played his hand and stuffed his pipe with Prince Albert tobacco. I loved that scent and always knew when Grampa was nearby—the wafts of Prince Albert arrived before he did. He was awesome. The problem was I also feared him, so I didn't dare seek his counsel. I kept my distance rather than risk crumbling under the power of that dreaded stare. I wish he'd lived longer; we would have been good friends.

Our next-door neighbor, Charlie, who was separated from us by only a thin driveway, was a mountain of a man. He was six-feet, eight-inches tall and easily three hundred pounds with a long, disheveled, gray beard, and bullying manner. You did not want to cross him. Rarely would he interact or talk to the neighborhood kids, and then he would only look at you with his dark eyes and grunt. When I became an adult I got to know him and he was a personable guy, but my first encounter was terrifying. I was in elementary school when a friend and I were trespassing in his dilapidated garage, which was really a falling-down, glorified shed where he stored old car parts and other junk. I was exploring a storage area that was on the second floor of the garage when my friend yelled up, "Somebody is coming!"

My friend flew the coop and I froze. I tried to hide behind some junk praying he would go away. No luck. He found me and he was pissed. Without muttering a word he grabbed me by the shirt collar and dragged me down the stairs, out of the garage, all the way to my front door, and delivered me to my mother with a simple yet calm message: "Keep him out of my garage."

I was so scared I pissed my pants. I vowed never to break and enter again.

My best friend as a preteen was a kid named Clarence. He was a year older than me, but he repeated first grade, so we were in the same class for a few years. Clarence and his mom, Mary, lived on Congress Street just a few houses down from Kellogg Street. Due to health issues, he was a small kid with poor vision and limited mobility, but I loved him. We would hang out playing board games in his room, or throwing a ball around in his driveway. His mom was a wonderful lady who babied Clarence and me whenever I was around. She had a boyfriend, his name was Ike, and he was a class act. Great people. I was sad when they moved away when I was twelve, and we lost touch. Today twelve-year-olds can text or tweet or stay connected on Facebook. In 1973, it was goodbye forever.

The Munjoy Hill of my youth in the '60s and '70s was considered by many, especially folks who didn't live on The Hill, the least desirable place to live in Portland. I enjoyed growing up there. Other than embarrassing run-ins with my father and the condition of our house, it was a fine place to grow up.

Portland itself was also ideal in many ways. It wasn't too big or too small. It was sizable enough to have authentic neighborhoods, a rich culture, and growing diversity, but not so big it was consumed by crime or sprawl. During my preteen years, all spent on Munjoy Hill, I was mostly naïve to the ills in the neighborhood around me. Even so, except for the rare road trip in Grampa's Opel to Foley's Ice Cream in Scarborough or to visit David or Marie after they left for Windham, my days were spent entirely within a mile radius of Kellogg Street. The car rides to Scarborough and Windham lasted only about twenty-five minutes, but to me it felt like they took forever. We didn't drive much (Ma never got a license or a car), so any travel seemed lengthy. I always got carsick. It didn't matter if it was five minutes or two hours, I was a motion-sickness mess.

Before Franklin Arterial was constructed, the neighborhood lines were more clearly conceded. For example, most kids living west of Washington Avenue and Mountfort Street went to different public elementary schools than those residing up on The Hill. Interaction was minimal if not at the Lee recreation center, the Boys Club, and the Ys. However, when the new four-lane road split Little Italy and Bayside in two, it changed the setting and perception of the neighborhood. Attending Cathedral School, which abuts the Arterial, for nine years and also playing Little League in Kennedy Park, made those areas feel like an extension of The Hill to me. Since I was born in 1961, and the Arterial is really all I've ever known, I tend to agree with those who consider everything east of Franklin Arterial as Munjoy Hill.

In its heyday, The Hill was primarily Irish, Italian, and Jewish immigrant families. By the time I arrived it was still an immigrant haven, but in decline. The Eastern Promenade remained stunning with its lavish lawns, grand homes, and open spaces. By contrast the rest of The Hill consisted of crowded aging multi-family homes and public housing. Contrasting smells filled the air daily. The pleasant early morning aromas emanating from John J. Nissen bakery on Washington Avenue and the B&M Baked Beans plant in East Deering would eventually, depending on wind direction, be overpowered by more ominous odors originating from Pine State By-Products in South Portland or the S.D. Warren Paper Mill in Westbrook. And boy was it loud. Whether it was the constant pounding of forging hammers at the Crosby Laughlin Plant on Fore Street or the clanking and whistles from the Grand Trunk rail cars making their way back and forth to the India Street terminal, it was always noisy.

Additionally, church bells tolled every hour, and there was seemingly incessant barking through neighborhoods devoid of a leash law. If peace and quiet was what you wanted, you didn't live on Munjoy Hill.

Naturally, the Eastern Prom was the most scenic spot in the East End. Bounded on three flanks by water, the Prom featured ball fields, tennis courts, and a playground on the northside of Congress Street. To the south were steep sweeping grasses, perfect for the annual Fourth of July celebration and picnics. In winter you couldn't find a better sledding spot. I'd occasionally dip in the pool overlooking the sea next to East End beach. Consequently, we got a lot of visitors. Many also flocked to the historic Portland Observatory, once a maritime signal tower, at the crest of the hill to climb its 103 steps, which on a clear day displayed incredible vistas of Casco Bay, and all the way to the White Mountains of New Hampshire. The fourth flank, the bottom of The Hill, rolled west into Little Italy and Kennedy Park, proceeding to the Old Port, Lincoln Park, and Bayside, before flattening out near prominent landmarks such as the Portland Press Herald building, City Hall, and Portland High School, and running into Monument Square and the retail district along Congress Street.

For the Irish, Italian, and Jewish families that populated Munjoy Hill in its glory days, money was scarce and spirits were diminished. Most families were large with loads of kids and extended family crowding into all available rooms. Not surprisingly, prominent societal ills of the time, primarily alcohol and drugs, were prevalent.

Certainly most of our neighbors around Kellogg Street struggled. Many lived below the poverty line, which was $4,000 a year for a family of four, yet a sense of community remained. Such nuances, plus the proliferation of mom-and-pop corner stores every few blocks, created a camaraderie and closeness. A fellow son of Munjoy Hill and Kellogg Street, Rick Dambrie, described the neighborhood this way: "Munjoy Hill was a place where those who lived there received a million dollar education in street smarts that didn't cost anything. The only thing you needed to pay was attention."

The sheer amount of people, sully situations, and potential pitfalls that we encountered daily pushed us to come of age quickly, or succumb to the strains.

Although I found Munjoy Hill a safe and suitable place to grow up, that was not the consensus in the community. In fact, Munjoy Hill was feared. The climate on The Hill was dark and stormy. The youth were considered hooligans, more interested in doing drugs and getting drunk than being good citizens. The Hill was infamous for The Corner. The Corner wasn't really a corner. It stretched a city block along Congress Street from North to Lafayette Streets. There were tenement buildings on the North Street end, while small local businesses, a laundromat and tailor shop, were situated near Lafayette Street. These homes and businesses were often vandalized. The tailor shop replaced broken windows on a regular basis. Across the street sat our local convenience store, the Nite Owl, which later became a Li'l Peach.

The Nite Owl was a traditional small convenience store, the approximate size of a Cumberland Farms store today. The only entry point was a set of double glass doors centered along the front of the building. Upon entering was a low-sitting candy and chip rack that separated the staff from the patrons. On each end of the rack two counters ran all the way to the back of the store. The register and the most common products to steal, like cigarettes, were always merchandised within this deep rectangle. On each side of the counters, shelving held the dry-good essentials. A walk-in cooler stretched along the back of the store.

When I worked at Li'l Peach in high school, I first observed the shady activities on The Corner. Local residents were afraid to shop at night due to frequent skirmishes in the area, plus the large crowds on The Corner were intimidating. By early evening mobs on The Corner spilled into the store parking lot. On any given night dozens, sometimes including one or two of my siblings, gathered on Congress Street from North to Lafayette, revving up for another night of drinking and drugs. The authorities were simply missing.

When I was older I wondered, "What chance did these kids have?"

Lost souls from good families adrift in a post-Woodstock haze on Munjoy Hill.

At home my mother implored us to stay away from The Corner and its drugs and alcohol. Some of my siblings ignored her, but for some reason, honestly, I don't know why, I listened. I'm sure I was scared. Naturally, my father's issues were top of mind and helped keep me somewhat grounded, and seeing firsthand what was happening to my friends was frightening. It's not that my mother wanted us off The Hill; she just wanted us to avoid what was dragging it down. In the end too many of my Munjoy Hill peers never found their way out.

The beauty of Ma was that she reinforced her relentless attacks on the troubles by threatening us with even more aggressive practical solutions. She believed education was the key to a successful future and a healthy distraction to the issues at home. That, and avoiding the popular vices of the day, would give us a chance to prosper. My mother didn't have all the answers, but she did have faith. In the end maybe we were just lucky, or perhaps God answered her prayers. I believe my mother's insistence on education, combined with kicking Walter out, greatly enhanced our well-being. That modeling probably would have fallen on deaf ears with a drunk around clouding up the picture and draining all hope.

On the streets, Walter often had a steady sidekick, Kicker. Like Walter, Kicker had a young family and would get "beer muscles" when on the sauce. He was big and strong, but often found trouble. One night in Lincoln Park he picked a fight with the wrong guy. The bum pulled out a hand axe and literally put a hole in his head. Kicker survived, but the battle scar left its mark. As a consequence of the blow, Kicker regularly had episodic seizures that seriously shortened his life.

Chapter Four
The Streets of Portland

In the fall of 1967, a priest was summoned to administer Last Rites to my father. It would happen five more times.

We can blame the first time on the Boston Red Sox. Walter loved the Sox. When he was sober, he rarely missed a game on the tube or radio. He even tried to schedule work, when he was actually employed, around game time. The Impossible Dream season of 1967 was magical in New England. That summer, the Red Sox, who had not had a winning season since 1958 and were coming off a last place finish in 1966, miraculously found themselves in the thick of the American League pennant race. It was glorious. And they won the pennant on the final day of the season, finishing one game ahead of both the Detroit Tigers and Minnesota Twins. That year, their dashing left fielder Carl "Yaz" Yastrzemski won the Triple Crown and became my favorite player. He was also my father's favorite; funny how that works when you are six.

In the World Series, Boston was matched against the St. Louis Cardinals. The Red Sox took the Redbirds the full seven games, but could not break through with a win against ace pitcher Bob Gibson. Gibson pitched and won games one, four, and seven, leading the Cards to the title. The loss was a crushing disappointment to Sox fans. The Sox hadn't appeared in a World Series since 1946, when Johnny Pesky infamously held the ball allowing the winning run to score, and had not won a title since 1918. Meanwhile, the hated New York Yankees had become a dynasty.

The game 7 loss to Gibson pushed Walter over the edge. He went on an epic drinking binge that landed him in a detox center—unconscious and nearly dead. The priest was summoned to give this former altar boy his Last Rites.

When raised Catholic, the seven sacraments drilled into your head are: Baptism, Communion, Penance, Confirmation, Marriage, Holy Orders, and Last Rites. Some, like Communion and Penance, are meant to be practiced habitually, while the sacraments of Baptism, Confirmation, Marriage, and Last Rites are meant to be received just once. A person only gets Last Rites when caretakers sense the end is near. Death is imminent so call the priest.

Walter didn't die. Somehow, he survived, but the scare didn't change his behavior.

In the '60s, I was too young or oblivious to truly grasp the extent of my father's drinking problem. However, by the early '70s I realized this homeless man was my father. I do remember him showing up at the house on occasion, getting something to eat and asking how we were, but that was random and rare at best. We had no relationship. My brother Walt, although just two-and-a-half years older, has some pleasant memories. Walt cherished our father's infrequent sober visits. Walt loved playing pass, watching games, and hearing his dad's voice. Even my older siblings, the Pauls, recall him as "a good guy" when sober and as a man who loved my mother. I think that spotlights Walter's biggest asset, he was so damn likable, and as a result most everyone suffered for him, and us. They knew when he was sober, it was only a matter of time before he'd relapse again.

My father was joined by a growing cast of characters who drifted around the streets of Portland. The neighborhoods from India Street west to High Street teemed with homeless men, predominantly alcoholics. Often, Walter even had at least one brother on the streets with him as well as numerous friends, like Kicker. Walter was on a first-name basis with the ladies who worked at the jail as well as many of the local cops. These relationships proved valuable, since the cops who liked him might let him sleep in an empty cell rather than freeze his ass off on a park bench or next to a nasty dumpster somewhere in the city.

His routines didn't change much in those days. On an average day he would wake up early, typically before dawn. If not in the jail, he was usually nestled up against a wall or tree, anywhere to keep warm and out of the wind. He would pull himself up and begin roaming the streets, bumming money for alcohol to relieve the pain that was already in his body. His first bottle of the day, usually Old Duke, both a personal favorite and a cheap option, was critical if for nothing else than to hold the nausea at bay. Even the cops knew the drill. On those nights when he bunked at the jail, the guards would often return his bottle to him on the way out in the morning. I guess they thought they were easing his pain. In a sense they were, because that is exactly what he craved. Walter always awoke "sick as a dog," and having a drink would settle and restore him.

Once he got that drink, he'd slip into an alley or along the waterfront looking for scraps of food or a secluded spot to catch a few more winks. By early afternoon he was already a walking zombie, bloated by cheap wine and oblivious to his surroundings.

If lucky, by nightfall, he could seize an unoccupied bed at the 24-Hour Club on India Street, the only shelter in Portland. (Still today at 65 India Street, Milestone Recovery provides services and

My dad during his homeless days. I found this picture at a flea market.

a safety net to our community's most vulnerable individuals who are struggling with chronic alcohol and drug dependence.) Unfortunately this indoor option rarely materialized for Walter since he was a night owl and because Portland, being a coastal city, checked in with chilly to cold evening temperatures nine months of the year and the limited number of beds at the 24-Hour Club filled early. Instead, he collected newspapers, cardboard boxes, and even trash for cover to stay warm. If he couldn't get warm, he just roamed the streets all night.

Eventually, all the sleeping outside turned Walter into an early riser. The sun didn't care, it rose bright and early each day. In truth, he didn't sleep much. He just napped on and off during the day, but he had to keep moving. If he tried to snooze in the park, the cops would shake him and tell him to move along. If he passed out in an alley, the business or homeowner would be rightly pissed and shoo him away. He tried to hide, but when your senses are shot you make poor decisions. He just crashed.

By nightfall he was so withered that, if turned away at the shelter, he'd pass out in the park or behind a building or other structure, often pissing and puking all over himself. Most mornings he'd drag his freezing, disgusting ass out from behind whatever cover he'd configured, drop by the 24-Hour Club to snag a complimentary six o'clock coffee, and start roving the city again.

At this point, he was in his 30s, but looked twice that age. He was unrecognizable; an aged man with a long, Gandalf-like salt-and-pepper beard and a long overcoat. He was mangy and ghastly. After getting his coffee he could have gone to the police gym and showered. That's what many of the Club dwellers—even those who missed out on a bunk—did after sleeping it off. Walter, apparently, never got that memo.

One rainy morning as Walter was leaving the Club, he noticed puddles forming in the gutters. He staggered along, his eyes pointed downward in despair. This was how the drunks moved about, head down; embarrassed and ashamed. He walked south to Commercial Street looking for handouts from the fisheries and other marine-related businesses that lined the street. He finally stopped at The Cut, his favorite local dive bar on the waterfront, to see if anybody was around to share or score a drink.

"Good morning, sunshine," a local fisherman called out. "Going to give us a hand?"

Walter would usually wave off the taunts, not feeling well, and in no mood to engage. Usually he avoided interacting with former friends and was uncomfortable running into folks who knew his kids. But sometimes that was unavoidable and old acquaintances called out, like Bobby.

"Walter, it's me Bobby. Come here, you look like hell."

"I'm not doing too good."

"Hey, your boy was over the house the other day. Real nice kid."

Although humiliated, Walter would instinctively hold out his hand hoping for a generous gift. Pride was no match for the need for money to buy that next drink.

"Thanks for being nice to my boy."

At times, he just stumbled along hoping for divine intervention, and on some mornings he received it. While staring blankly down he'd glimpse something floating in a puddle or some money pressed up against a building. Paranoid and nervously questioning his good fortune he'd cry out, "Thank you, Jesus," as he picked up the money off the ground. Windfall in hand, he'd quickly make his way to a package store for wine and cigarettes. If a lucky bill didn't divinely develop, Walter would panhandle to score enough dough to buy what he needed. If panhandling didn't work fast enough, he resorted to shoplifting. From dawn to dusk Walter worked the streets of Portland looking for money or a place to pass out. That in a nutshell was his daily life.

It is truly amazing how many people in downtown Portland "looked after" my father. At times police officers, attorneys, and shop owners surprised Walter with a gift, usually food or a few bucks. He was arguably the most well-liked and, as insane as it sounds, respected bum in town. For the most part Walter was a happy drunk, nice and respectful to folks.

Any good bum knows some places are better than others and my father spent countless hours moving in and around Monument

Square since the pickings there were ripe. Lawyers and government officials would exit their workplace and see Walter at the ready, tin cup extended. Many of these professionals knew the family and were always gracious. When hungry Walter would scrounge the back alleys for scraps. The owner and staff of George's Deli in the heart of Monument Square were especially kind-hearted.

One summer day, Walter parked himself on the stoop at the James Bailey Company Sporting Goods store. The clerk needed him to move.

"Mr. Crockett, I'm sorry you can't stay here on the stoop. You have to move along."

As Walter pulled himself up and prepared to relocate, the clerk asked him, "Walter, where's your hat? You need a hat."

The clerk pulls a new Red Sox cap from behind his back and fits it onto Walter's head.

"There you go, that's much better."

As Walter walked away, the clerk closed with, "Mr. Crockett, be safe."

A Boston Red Sox cap was probably his most prized possession in those days.

One of Walter's other favorite panhandling spots was Lincoln Park. Located slightly east of Downtown, Lincoln Park sat adjacent to the police station, fire station, and several federal buildings. A few blocks away were several legal offices, the Portland Press Herald, and Portland High School. Basically, Lincoln Park was a gold mine for a crafty panhandler. And, conveniently, there was a package store across from the park. Occasionally, the police came through to sweep the park clean of Walter and his fellow winos, forcing them to search for other spots.

Commercial Street, right along Casco Bay from India Street to High Street, was also very popular. Walter could always count on the seafaring crowd to help him out. Not just with money, but also leftovers. The food scraps from the seafood restaurants probably kept him from starving to death for years.

Another hot spot, and probably even the quickest buck, was the corner of High and Congress streets and the Eastland Hotel. At the time, this ritzy hotel was where the well-heeled boarded, and their packed pockets were profitable to the panhandler. It was also the prime spot for Portland's prostitution trade, which proved handy when the begging proved profitable and a downtrodden drunk was feeling frisky. It didn't cost much for a hand job or blow job back in the day.

The streets were not necessarily peaceful. There were many confrontations amongst the bums. Fights, both verbal and physical, were the norm and my father never backed down. He was friendly to his panhandling targets and shopkeepers, but not so much to those living on the streets with him. Even though he had become a shadow of the man he was when boxing, everyone else was frail too. It was a fair fight. The word is that Walter didn't start many fights, but he ended most of them. Most arguments were about stupid stuff. Some panhandlers tried to claim specific spots around the city as their own. In truth, there were no such rules, and it was "first come, first get" for the prime spots. But trespass on a perceived territory and sparks would fly. During baseball season Red Sox-versus-Yankees arguments also led to a lot of disagreements and tussles.

Fights were one thing, but what really hurt was getting rolled.

The genuine bums like my father were frequently passed out and Walter got mugged many times. If he wore a warm jacket or Red Sox cap and passed out in the open, they were often long gone when he woke.

The only change in his rinse and repeat existence was detox. If the cops picked him up and he seemed in especially dire straits, they would cart him off to a detox center somewhere in New England. There is no question that these forced weeks of sobriety helped keep him alive longer than would otherwise have happened. In the aftermath, he attended some AA meetings. But that never lasted long.

The reasons for his stays were always eerily similar. Walter would drink to the point of being unable to stand or communicate. The police would scrape Walter off the street, haul him to the local jail, and send him to the nearest detox facility. When it came to detox, Walter had personal circumstances working in his favor. First and foremost he was a veteran, which gave him access to the Togus VA Medical Center in Augusta as well as other detox centers and hospitals in New England. The second thing working in his favor was being a Catholic. Since many detox centers were supported and run by Catholic Charities, the church cared for the broken bums and put the drunks to work, once they dried out.

When local shelters were full, drunks were shipped south to the nearest vacant detox facility. Walter recuperated at multiple centers in and around Boston. In downtown Boston, there was a Catholic Charities dormitory where he'd stay and, when finally able, be put to work. The church would supply shelter and food, plus a job paying five to ten dollars a week depending on how much you could do.

In moments of sobriety, he often worked on trucks moving furniture, papers, or anything else Catholic Charities staffers needed to consign. At the time there were many Catholic Charity stores in Massachusetts, so work was steady. Walter thought it was a good deal—at least until he felt better and bolted.

At other times, once Walter was deemed healthy and functioning properly, he'd simply walk away from the shelter. Free again, he chose one of two options: immediately start drinking again or get back to Portland and try to stay sober.

During one sober stretch, he stopped at our house to watch the Red Sox with us. What happened is the one memory I have of my father inside our house. We were enjoying the game when suddenly Walter was on the floor shaking uncontrollably. I had no idea what the hell was going on; he was frothing at the mouth and trembling violently. We were stunned. I was freaking out thinking my father was going to die right in front of my eyes. My mother raced in, got him to sit up and Carolyn called MEDCU, the paramedic rescue ambulatory service run by the Portland Fire Department.

By the time the medics arrived he was breathing normally, but still quivering. He had suffered a frightening episode of delirium tremens or DTs, in our living room. DTs, also known as the rum fits, were common for my father and other skid row bums. The body can only handle so much alcohol before revolting and telling the addict to cut the shit.

His chair and folding table were strewn all over the room, plates and glassware splintered on the floor, as the dogs rushed in to fight over the fallen food. It was sheer chaos. Fortunately, my mom had seen this before and knew what to do.

To this point in my young life I'd never had a drink. I was told point blank by my mother that if I had even one drop of alcohol this could be my fate. "You will be just like your father!"

Walter was afraid of the fits since most of his delusions were chilling. He'd hear strange voices and people plotting to hurt him. He dreaded the horrors and knew they only happened when he was sobering up. By his logic, the best way to avoid them was to not sober up. To me, down at my most skeptical level, it felt like a choice. I was too young to realize it was a disease.

Once in the early '70s, Water was arrested for public intoxication in Portland. After appearing in court he was sentenced to ten days in the county jail and the guards escorted him to a small padded cell in the bowels of the jail. A few days into his stay, he went into the horrors. Much of what he saw in his mind was senseless and harmless, but some of the scenes were macabre. He saw himself killed or maimed in his visions. But he also held his own private concert. Musicians walked through the walls with instruments in hand singing songs and encouraging Walter to join them. Naturally, he did, crooning at the top of his lungs, only taking a break when exhaustion knocked him out.

Guards watched in stunned silence as Walter fell to his knees, hands raised and clasped, bellowing,

> *Must I forever be a beggar*
> *Whose golden dreams will not come true?*
> *Or will I go from rags to riches?*
> *My fate is up to you.*

And, then he talked to the walls, crying, "Whadda ya mean you can't help me? You're all I've got."

And suddenly he was singing again, belting out Elvis' "Jailhouse Rock" and the Beatles' "Let It Be" before again passing out.

When he finally escaped the horrors, he didn't know where he was or what had happened.

A guard opened the cell door and asked, "How are you feeling this morning, Walter?"

"I'm awful tired, what's going on?"

The guard knew the horrors were over, since he wasn't talking gibberish. Once they passed, the jail transferred him into a cell with four or five other guys to run out the sentence.

On the way to the group cell Walter asked the guard, "Was I in the padded cell overnight?"

"No," said the guard, "you were down there five nights."

Walter just hung his head, "Sorry."

Chapter Five
Ma and Me

While Walter wasted away on the streets of Portland, Ginny focused on raising her children. I have learned something from everyone close to me—grandparents, parents, siblings, family, and friends. All have contributed to the man I am today, good and bad. But nobody had a greater effect on me, deep down in my heart and soul, than my mother. Ma was compassionate and selfless. She always offered people a thoughtful gift or sympathetic word. She never forgot a birthday or anniversary. She was loyal, arguably to a fault. Although she struggled with her health, she was bright and thrifty, which proved essential since we didn't have much. Even though her methods were unconventional, to say the least, she kept pushing us forward. She *always* wanted better for us, stressing that we could be anything we wanted to be.

She would confuse me, urging me to "do as I say, not as I do," and on the flip side urging me to lead by example. I often pointed out this oxymoron, but she stubbornly stuck to her guns. It was always tough to use logic with Ma. She seemed fully cognizant of her faults even if she completely ignored them. She knew she set a poor example, but she was determined that we break the family cycle.

My siblings in the early 1960s. Clockwise from top left: Jimmy, David, Gin, Marie, Danny, Me, Walt, and Carolyn.

Almost daily, she hammered on the following virtues: faith, loyalty, and, most importantly, education. We all went to parochial schools; to her the public school system was not an option, at least until high school, and then only grudgingly. She had an unflinching devotion to Catholicism and believed it provided the best education. It cost money to attend the parochial schools, but since we were broke and the family was active in the church, Cathedral parish never pressed Ma for tuition. All eight of her children attended those elementary and junior high schools.

She may have been devout, but I don't give the Catholic Church much credit for my growth or success. This is not a knock on the church or parochial school education, but rather an homage to my mother. I believe education starts at home and must be reinforced there. Church and school can certainly shape and encourage you, but if the work isn't supported at home it simply won't stick. It is a fact that poverty and alcoholism can repeat themselves generation after generation, especially if there is no role model at home or, even worse, poor role models who set bad examples.

We all need guidance, especially young people, so when positive examples aren't present, maybe a little more from the adults would help. Trust me, I understand it's not as simple as "do as I say, not as I do," but I witnessed too many great kids from The Hill, who received little to no support at home, repeat the same missteps as their parents. It is real and it is a damn hard cycle to break.

My mother was a high school graduate. College wasn't an option for her. She was the oldest child and had to help support the family. I don't know where she got the idea that a college education was critical to success and the best way off The Hill, but she sold it as gospel, right along with her faith. I certainly benefited from watching my seven older siblings experiment with different paths to success and happiness and failure. By the time I came along, college wasn't just a possible option, it was an expectation. However, her idea of education wasn't only about books and schoolwork. It was also about handling life and its challenges. Ma and I talked frequently about the issues that surrounded us, including those right in our own home—poverty, alcohol, and drugs. All were prevalent on Munjoy Hill throughout my youth. Ma believed hard work and an education, along with faith and a clear plan, could beat the odds.

When I was young, I assumed food stamps, or funny money as I called them, were real money. I'd go to the market with my mother, and when she handed the cashier food stamps she would often get change in cash. It took time before I comprehended that the two forms of currency were not interchangeable. Food stamps came with a social stigma attached. The rules were puzzling, because there were certain products, like cat and dog food, that you couldn't buy with food stamps. Once I knew what using

food stamps meant, transactions at the store could be embarrassing to me. I was confused and recall moving through the checkout
lane fearful about creating a scene. I had to separate what we were
allowed to purchase with food stamps versus what we were not.
Whenever I made a mistake, I'd want to hide, because it seemed
the store clerk was purposely trying to make me feel *really* small. It
sucked. But for the most part Ma sheltered me from such humilia-
tion. I was sensitive to the stigma and she did her best to shield me.
I would wait outside while she bought the groceries and faced the
music alone. Of course, I made quick runs to the store that sometimes included funny money, but more often than not, she gave me
cash.

It wasn't just the food stamps. As I grew older, I was keenly
aware of being poor and embarrassed by it. When I started junior
high, I was in desperate need of a winter coat. The state of Maine
funded winter coats for families in need. Since Ma was not
working and Walter was out of the picture, our family qualified
for maximum welfare benefits, which included the winter coat
program. The downside to the coat program was that the state
issued only one style of coat to *all* the families who qualified. That
made it *very* easy to pick out the haves and have-nots. I certainly
appreciated the warm coat, but wearing the coat felt degrading and
created immediate problems. A handful of businesses around town
were selected to distribute the coats, and most of the establishments
contributed to the blatant stereotyping by offering the same coat.

My mother found an exception in a store owner who listened,
understood the problem, and was willing to work with her. Levinsky's, a retail clothing store, was located on Congress Street right
across from the Cathedral School. The owner was a kind man who
had known my mother for years. He had hired my sister Gin and
was acquainted with all the family. He was also familiar with my

father, since his store was located between two of Walter's regular spots, the 24-Hour Club and Lincoln Park. In fact, he chased a panhandling Walter away from the front of his store on numerous occasions. In short, he knew the Crocketts.

Ma knew about my embarrassment and remembered the harassment that came my way while wearing the "welfare kid coat" the previous winter. She knew because I reminded her, "Ma, I'm not going through it again; I'd rather freeze."

Granted my stand wasn't the brightest, since I needed a coat, but I was young and stubborn and it was a hill I was ready to die on—figuratively speaking. After Ma stepped in, the store owner agreed to let her pay for any difference between the cost of a welfare coat and the cost of a different one. So, when we got to the store, the owner took me aside and offered me alternative styles. I was thrilled to wear a non-welfare kid coat that year. My choice wasn't very chic (two-toned pink and gray), nonetheless it was different, and that was all that mattered.

My mother never did understand how money really worked, but she wanted to instill in me the value of saving and using it wisely. I was in high school when she first asked me to prepare her taxes. Doing my mother's taxes was easy; it only took a few lines. We would sit down at the kitchen table, spread out the paperwork and dive in. She handed me the statement that indicated her annual income—it showed less than $3,000.

"Is this right, is this all you get?" I asked.

"Yes, and it's the most I've ever received."

I was blown away. How did she support herself and up to eight children on less than $3,000? In fairness, she also received food stamps monthly to supplement her income and my grandparents provided occasional support, but they certainly weren't wealthy either. Still, I have no idea how she managed. Well, I guess I do. We simply went without and I didn't take stock in what I did or didn't have. I trusted she was doing her best. Sure I was gullible and forgiving, but I took her message to heart: "Do as I say, not as I do."

Ma often referred to me as "House Devil, Street Angel."

I suppose it was somewhat accurate, but I never really thought the tag fit. Basically she asserted that I was well-behaved at school, church and anywhere in public, but that my behavior at 60 Kellogg Street was not good; in fact it was devilish. Was I mouthy at times? Yes, but not excessively so. I considered it another one of Ma's religious adages that she preached to us constantly, hoping they would take.

As part of that, one erroneous message I received as a youth was that everything was a sin. I'm convinced that I was a late bloomer because of her off-the-wall declarations. For example, according to Ma, drinking alcohol was a sin. I guess considering her ties to alcoholics, I had empathy for her position even if she was extreme.

It did slow my social development. Early on in my life, I drew a proverbial line in the sand regarding drinking, and chose to stay home rather than go out with friends and have a pop or two. It took me a while to loosen up socially.

Another huge sin to Ma was sex. Any kind of sex. Masturbation, oral sex, pre-marital sex. She felt even thinking about sex was sin. As an adolescent, I didn't know what to think. Maybe it was all the pent-up frustration that made me a "house devil." No, that probably wasn't it; I was rather fresh. However, knowing her real-life background and just pondering her "Do as I say, not as I do" motto and her list of sins still makes me smile.

Regardless of her complexities, Ma was more afraid of the toll that could be taken by alcohol and drugs than anything else in this world. She saw firsthand what it did to her second husband and to her father. She truly believed there was a "drinker gene" that infected our family, and she was convinced that all it took was a single drink to kick in. From the moment she booted Walter in 1963, you couldn't find a drop of alcohol or tobacco in our house. Ma never drank and she never smoked. She didn't even want it around her. Nobody drank or smoked in her house, although certainly some of her children were doing so elsewhere or in secret.

As a result of all this, I really don't know what it is like to grow up actually *living* in a house with an alcoholic. But I do know what it was like when one looms over everything that happens. As I have said, my dad was *the* symbol of sin and failure that my mother held up before me as a warning. With the fervor of an evangelist, she preached to me: "If you drink you'll end up just like your father—out on the streets."

Deep down, whether I knew it or not, I took that to heart. I had a deep-seated fear that I might end up like him. That pressure bubbled over when I was in elementary school and I banked the first ugly memory of my father.

Although Walter was kicked out of the family home when I was an infant, he occasionally visited when sober and tried to play nice. I don't remember those visits, but I do recall when he'd show up smashed. Ma tried to prepare us for these unwanted visits with her classic line: "No matter what, don't let the cats out and don't let Walter in."

I suppose it was good to know that my father didn't rate any higher than us when it came to the cats. Those times when he staggered up to the house unexpectedly featured a lot of drama between my parents on the front steps. I suppose it was entertaining for the neighbors, but it really sucked for us. One chilly spring Sunday evening in 1971, he arrived at the door all liquored up and disheveled.

My sister Gin on the steps of 60 Kellogg Street.

Prior to his arrival it had been a fun day. After Mass, my friend Clarence and I played pass on the street and I was excited to show off my new red baseball glove. I keenly remember everything about that glove because it was the only piece of sporting equipment I ever owned that wasn't a hand-me-down. I was playing farm-league baseball for the first time that summer and I needed a glove. Ma saw it in a markdown bin, and knowing red was my favorite color, she picked it up. It didn't have much padding and was a tad small, but it was original.

As the day grew colder, Clarence and I moved inside and I bored him to death, I'm sure, going through my regular Sunday routine of determining the current MVPs of the American and National Leagues. My grandparents always got the *Maine Sunday Telegram*. When they finished they would give me the sports section and I'd devour all the stats. Every week I'd grab a piece of paper and pencil and write down the league leaders in the printed categories (hits, doubles, triples, home runs, runs batted in, and batting average) and assign a point system.

For example, if a player was leading the league in home runs he received one point. I did this for each category and listed the top ten for each stat, and assigned the point totals from one to ten. If the ballplayer didn't make the list in a specific category he was assigned an eleven. After gathering all the information I added up each player's total and the all-star with the fewest points was declared league MVP for that week. This always took a few hours, so Clarence usually stayed for dinner. I'm convinced doing all that adding, subtracting, and occasional multiplying freed me from any fear of mathematics.

Thank God it was a Sunday since that was the only day of the week we had a family dinner. With everyone's schedules all over the map, it was a challenge to get most of us to sit down together and break bread. Dinner usually consisted of white rice, pasteurized yellow cheese (it came in a long block), and powdered milk, all compliments of the state of Maine. When Ma really wanted to spice things up she'd add a can of cream of mushroom soup and smother it all over the white rice. It was delicious. If we were being really good we might get some fried bologna cups.

After dinner we always watched "Mutual of Omaha's Wild Kingdom" and "The Wonderful World of Disney." It was during "Wild Kingdom" that we heard a loud knock on the front door. Ma went to the door and found Walter crouched over the porch railing. Pulling the curtain aside from behind the locked door Ginny shouted, "Walter, what are you doing here? You can't even stand up."

"No, no, Ginny. I'm good."

She tapped on the window trying to get his attention.

"Look at me. You can't be here. You're drunk. You need to leave, NOW."

Ginny closed the curtain and went back inside. Walter rattled the whole house as he continued banging on the front door. The commotion was a huge distraction, so I asked Ma, "What's all the racket out there?"

"Nothing, just some ruckus on the street."

But clearly flustered she added, "Boys, it's getting late, sorry to cut the night short, but time to go home," and she drifted into the kitchen to call the cops.

The banging kept getting louder and louder.

After calling the cops, Ma flew to the front door. Clarence and I shrugged and followed her into the foyer. Walt and Carolyn were now peering into the hall as well.

Ma pulled the curtain aside and rapped on the window to get Walter's attention.

"Walter, you need to leave, right now! I called the cops."

"Oh, come on, Ginny. It's fucking freezing out here. You know I have nowhere to go, just let me in."

Ma didn't budge. She shook her head and went back into the apartment. She walked right past us.

There are dozens of other instances over the years when my mother, grandfather, grandmother, or even older siblings would stand on the porch trying to reason with a drunken Walter, encouraging him to move on. I'm not sure what possessed me, but on this particular night I confronted my father at the front door.

I started screaming at him.

"Dad! Go away! Just go away! Go away!"

"Let me in, I'm your father. Open this door, noooooooow!"

I started to cry. With tears in my eyes, I screamed at my father again.

"No! Just go away. GO AWAY!"

The exchange was fairly brief. We yelled a few more unpleasantries at each other and then he was gone, stumbling down the stairs just ahead of the police sirens. Clarence and my siblings were stunned.

After Clarence left the house, my brother admonished me.

"How could you do that to Dad?"

I still feel guilty about this altercation. My outburst presented Ma with a conundrum. She was proud of me, but really couldn't show it. She did a nice job of calming me down and suggested I go to confession if I was feeling bad about it, which I did.

I didn't want to do it, but my mother was at the end of her rope, and if my father didn't leave he'd be arrested and once again we'd watch him get dragged away. I know I embarrassed him and hurt him. But he left.

Walt and me hanging the family stockings in the early 1970s.

Chapter Six
Faith

There is no question that when I was a teenager, I suffered from cumulative religious overload. Eleven years of parochial school with mandatory religious education classes everyday, plus serving as an altar boy into high school was spiritual overkill. We were expected to be at church every Sunday and all forty days of Lent. Yes, every day for forty straight days. Ma's message was as sinister as it was direct: "It's a sin if you don't go to Mass every week and every day during Lent." I learned later that she was exaggerating, but try telling her that. She wouldn't hear of it.

My mother always claimed, "My faith never let me down, while most everything else did." I believe part of her wished that she had actually become a nun as she considered when a teenager. She wished the church had just taken her away. After all, her husbands were both losers, she suffered from poor health, and she lacked confidence. Still, she never lost faith.

As a result of her faith and devotion, Cathedral school and church were my homes away from home from kindergarten through eighth grade, which means into the mid-1970s. I was fond of a few teachers like Sister Conrad and Sister Mona, and the unforgettable Sisters Elsa and Edward Mary in seventh grade, and my favorite, Sister Thaddene in eighth grade. In my nine years at

Cathedral, I never had a lay teacher, and there was scarcely a male teacher to be found.

I loved everything about Cathedral School. The uniform was easy. Boys wore a blue button-down shirt and a plaid tie with slacks and shoes. Everybody was similar so nobody made fun of your clothes (well, mostly not). Classes were small, maybe fifteen students per class, and spread out over the two brick buildings. Kindergarten through sixth grades were together in the grammar school on Locust Street, while the junior high school was across the schoolyard next to the church. I was a diligent student which made schoolwork manageable. We endured religious education classes daily, and were expected to participate at church as an altar boy, in the choir, or both.

The Cathedral complex took up an entire city block bordered by Congress Street, Franklin Arterial, Cumberland Avenue, and Locust Street. Cathedral Grammar School was one of only two properties on its side of Locust Street. The entrances to Cathedral Junior High and the Cathedral of the Immaculate Conception faced Cumberland Avenue, while the parish rectory and Guild Hall looked out on Congress Street.

School through third grade was mundane. I was shy and didn't talk much, and the school didn't offer any sports teams. As a result, every day featured the same routine. We would gather each morning in the schoolyard (the pavement between the grammar school and junior high) waiting for the bell. When it rang, we queued up in single file with our teacher. We'd have morning classes, followed by recess (always in the schoolyard when the weather permitted), more classes, lunch, then back to classes until we were finally dismissed and walked home.

The highlight of the day was definitely lunch. We ate lunch every day at the Guild Hall, which for an elementary schooler was a bit of a hike. Although it was only a few hundred yards it seemed a lot longer to me. Maybe because we were supposed to be on our best behavior while walking to the Guild Hall since the Lord was *watching your every step*. There wasn't a day that our teachers didn't threaten us with no lunch if we didn't behave. Naturally we'd horse around with our classmates, keeping the nuns on their toes, from the time we left the classroom until we planted our seats on the cafeteria-style table benches that were lined from end to end in the big hall.

The Guild Hall's facade was impressive. The wide, steep stone steps centered in the building seemed to thunder, "This is a very important place!" It really did feel special walking into the Guild Hall. Breakfast and lunch was served daily. School plays, banquets, and special events were performed on the stage, and Bingo filled the room most nights for older parishioners and friends. Given our financial limitations, I ate a free breakfast and lunch at the Guild Hall whenever school was in session. In fact, I was introduced to my favorite drink, whole milk, at the Guild Hall. It was from Locust Farm. I told myself that it had been delivered by my Uncle Brud since he was still employed by the dairy.

The Cathedral of the Immaculate Conception was a refuge for many of us, especially if you were an altar boy or in the choir.

I remember getting all dressed up to receive my first communion and confession, and being confirmed. Of course we had to practice for weeks to make sure we had the ceremonies down pat. Rehearsing for the Stations of the Cross or other school services tied us up for hours on end.

Nothing occupied time like being an altar boy. I was an altar boy from as far back as I can remember. It was gratifying and an important responsibility. Walt and I were often assigned to Mass together, and that was exciting for Ma. She sat in her pew beaming from ear to ear. Altar-serving at my sister Gin's wedding was without doubt my most memorable call to duty.

I don't recall sitting in a pew at the Cathedral until graduation. It seemed like I was assigned to serve Mass every week, all special occasions, and daily during Advent and Lent. At least the church was stunning. Both long and wide, under a fifty-foot raised ceiling accentuated by statues of holy men and gargoyles, swept mahogany pews, Roman columns, and startling stained-glass windows. Throw in the marble altar, pious garb, red wine, and mega-sized organ with its accompanying acoustics, you had no choice but to respect the setting. I even got to ring the church bell a few times, significant since it was suspended in the steeple at the very top of the church, topped by a cross that skied to Portland's highest structural point. Once I was a little too close to the bell, and my ears literally rang for days.

One of the opportunities afforded to me by the church that I'm most thankful for was two weeks of summer camp. For nearly fifty years the Archdiocese operated camps for young Catholic boys, Camp Gregory in Gray, and for girls, Camp Pesky (Pesquasawasis) in Poland, free of charge. Starting around the early 1970s, every summer Walt and I got shipped to Camp Gregory on the grounds of Saint Gregory's Church. We'd pack a duffel bag, drag it to the Cathedral schoolyard, and catch the bus for the ride to Gray. We always had a few schoolmates with us; it was a great adventure. The property was cool. Set on Crystal Lake, the cabins were all triangular in design with about a dozen cots in each. A half-wall separated us from our lone counselor. (No privacy here; I felt right at home.) It was rise and shine with the morning bell and a race over to the mess hall for breakfast. From there it was a plethora of activities. Every game imaginable was available, including some I'd never heard of before like tetherball. Slapping at that ball for hours, trying to avoid getting smacked in the head, was a blast. Another activity I tried for the first and only time at camp was archery. The archery field was located at the far end of the property bordering the main road heading toward Gray center. This proved to be good local knowledge whenever we'd sneak off the grounds to buy some penny candy and a soda pop at the Dry Mills store about a mile up the road.

The arts and crafts activities were the best. I had never heard of or seen gimp before going to camp. Gimp is a flat or round plastic string used in crafts. It came in a variety of colors and could be braided, knotted, or woven into bracelets, key chains or even lanyards. You could get very creative and elaborate with this stuff. I remember making a blue-and-white (Cathedral colors) bracelet for myself and more imaginative projects, like necklaces, for my family.

We spent hours in the water. Maine is blessed with over 2,500 lakes and Crystal Lake, although relatively small, didn't disappoint. Known for its year-round fishing, it offered ample rainbow, brown, and brook trout in its waters. The state stocks the lake annually with these three species to sustain their populations.

The first day at camp featured mandatory swim testing. This "test" always stressed me out. I never took formal swim lessons and wasn't confident in the water. Depending on how you did on your test you were assigned to one of the zones: Dolphins, for beginners or those who couldn't swim; Barracudas, for average swimmers; and Sharks, for strong swimmers. If you were a Dolphin, you were not allowed to enter the Barracuda or Shark zones. I never advanced beyond Dolphin. Initially, I couldn't swim at all so that was the right place for me. Over time I taught myself to swim, kind of. I could get from point A to point B, but refused to put my face in the water while swimming. The instructors told me: "No Barracuda and definitely not Shark until you swim properly."

I grew to enjoy my fellow Dolphins.

Evenings at camp were always fun. Nightly campfires with stories about creepy three-fingered Willy always entertained, and the s'mores were outstanding. One summer the councilors decided to hold boxing matches. I wasn't interested, but Walt was all over it. He idolized Muhammad Ali and looked forward to showing off his moves. He believed he could float like a butterfly, sting like a bee, and shuffle his feet like the great heavyweight. The day of the bouts my close friend and Cathedral classmate, Kevin, asked me to fight this bully that had been picking on him. I was like, "Why don't you kick his ass?" I could tell he was scared, and, like me, he wasn't a fighter. I'm not sure why he thought I could take this kid, but he managed to guilt me into trying.

The fights were scheduled for three one-minute rounds and Walt was the first one up. I don't recall whom he fought, but I do remember him dancing around like a clown for three minutes. The other guy couldn't land a punch, Walt got a few good jabs in, and won by unanimous decision. Now I was starting to get really nervous. I didn't know how to box and what if this kid kicked my ass? I'd be the laughingstock of the camp, or at least my family. We were in one of the last bouts, and I considered following Walt's lead and just dancing around for three minutes. I quickly realized I wasn't in good enough shape to do that and found myself squaring off in the center of the ring. Somehow, my right hand connected to his left cheek and he went down. I don't think I really hurt him, he was the stereotypical bully who stayed down once he got punched in the face. I was pretty happy though. Winning the fight by technical knockout was much more impressive than by unanimous decision. Either way, I felt our father would have been proud.

After I yelled at my father on our front porch, I went to confession as Ma suggested and the priest absolved me. Still, I couldn't shake it.

I'd see my father loitering around the Cathedral complex when I was coming or going from church and school, but I never acknowledged him. Unbeknownst to me, he would lurk in the shadowy alley between Levinsky's and the Superette across from school and watch me play. All the years on the streets left Walter weak. He didn't eat well and his mostly liquid diet had caused the former muscular middleweight boxer to shrivel to nearly one hundred pounds.

The owners of DiPietro's Sandwich Shop on Cumberland Avenue and Amato's Italian Sandwiches on India Street had empathy for the broken and gave him some food that helped him survive. Both businesses were located in Portland's "Little Italy" and DiPietro's was across the street from Cathedral Grammar School. By now my father, who had been homeless and drunk for more than a decade, was in a deep-rooted daze and subsisted as a "shadow" to his family. But he remained an artful dodger. When his faculties permitted he would duck away, never wanting to confront us near the Cathedral block. Every schoolday I walked down Congress Street, dodging the bullies at North School, past India Street to Cathedral School and never saw my father. I might get a rare glimpse of him lying in wait near DiPietro's during recess, or in Lincoln Park while getting my free breakfast or lunch at the Guild Hall, which sat diagonal to the park. To his credit, if he saw kids coming his way he'd make a beeline out of sight so as not to embarrass us. I appreciated the effort. There was nothing more humiliating than facing your drunken, homeless father in front of your classmates.

Most of my elementary and junior high school age memories are sports-related or involve some other form of competition. Cathedral kids were resourceful. We concocted games at recess that used our brick surroundings. Two noteworthy games were sockball and fallout shelter. In sockball we would take old socks, round them up into a ball, then stitch our creation shut to keep it intact, basically a softer baseball. The teachers were fine with sockballs since they were less likely to break things, principally windows. Your arm and palm served as the bat. The hitter would await the pitch and swing away. We usually played automatics, but sometimes we'd run the bases. Unlike baseball where I was afraid of the ball, I had no fear of the sockball. We also used the sockball to play fallout shelter. The name came from the signs that were posted on the school buildings. If there was a bomb threat, students were to go single file to the basement of the school—the fallout shelter. We used the fallout shelter signs as baskets. We would play man-to-man, physical defense, while trying to score the sockball in the round circle that was at the heart of the fallout shelter sign. The signs were perfectly placed about eight feet above the ground. The games got spirited, some fights occasionally broke out, but overall it was a good time. My father watched me play these games from afar.

I tried out for Little League when I was ten and got placed on a farm league team. Admittedly, I was not a good baseball player. Watching me try to judge a fly ball was comical, and my trying to hit the baseball with my eyes closed never went well. Being afraid of the ball relegated me to the outfield, usually for two innings each game, for the entirety of my three-year Little League career. My farm league coach, Mr. Wing, gave me a chance in the infield, but after watching me pirouette away from every ground ball, he sent me to right field. However, I do recall one highlight. While in the majors I was patrolling center field when the league's best slugger came up and hit a shot to dead center. I raced back to the chain-link fence and stuck my red glove into the air and miraculously the ball landed and stayed in the pocket, and we won the game. The red glove, not me, saved the day.

Little League 5, consisting of both farm and major leagues, was played in Kennedy Park. Kennedy Park was rough and the kids were tough. I knew many of them since they attended North Elementary School on Congress Street. Deciding to play Little League meant I'd have to again work to dodge the bullies from North School, only this time on their home turf. That was downright frightening. Dealing with home-field advantage and no teachers to break up the ruckus wasn't something I wanted to contemplate. So I either walked through Kennedy Park with a big group from the Hill, or I went the long way around via Fox Street to the playing fields.

My favorite memory of Little League had nothing to do with game action. One year, my farm league team, Soule Glass, won the league championship. After our last game, Mr. Wing took us to the Dairy Bar on the corner of Washington and Cumberland avenues to celebrate. We didn't get trophies in those days, even for winning the league title.

Mr. Wing said: "Boys, congratulations. Order anything you'd like."

This rattled me a bit since I'd never had a treat other than an ice cream cone. I stepped back to see what the other kids were ordering before moving to the window and asking for a banana split. Confusion set in when the guy behind the counter asked me what flavors and toppings I wanted. I didn't realize there were choices. I said, "Can I have it like in the picture?" which was taped on the window. When he came back with this huge ice cream monstrosity, I was happier than a pig in shit. I always thought Mr. Wing was a good coach, but this celebration elevated him to the best ever.

It was right around the age I began Little League that Cathedral offered its one and only sport, basketball. Cathedral had two teams, a fifth- and sixth-grade team and a seventh- and eighth-grade team. Both teams played at the Portland Boy's Club against St. Patrick's, St. Joseph's, and the Baxter School for the Deaf. With only four teams in the league, we became well-acquainted. I was a good basketball player. I developed my skills playing regularly at the Munjoy South basketball court. During the summer, the neighborhood kids played pickup for hours. The games were competitive and friendly. (I still play pickup ball today and chuckle when the young adults bitch the whole time. I ask myself, "Is this the seventh game of the NBA finals?" Maybe it's me, but I don't remember every game, or even possession, circa 1970s, turning into a bitch session.)

When I was in fourth grade, Cathedral's fifth- and sixth-grade basketball team was short on numbers so the coach decided to add a fourth-grader. Tryouts for the additional spot were held at the basketball court inside the Guild Hall. Looking at Guild Hall from the outside you'd never envision a full court with adjacent locker rooms anywhere in the building, never mind in the basement. The court had one unique characteristic that likely affected every basketball player who ever came out of Cathedral—the ceiling was only a few feet above the backboard. As a result my jump shot was pretty flat—and I prided myself on being a shooter. You were forced to shoot near line drives or risk having the ball scrape the ceiling. Since we never played real games there, it didn't really matter, but many Cathedral Knights players perfected their own line-drive jumper. A handful of us fourth-graders tried out and I made the

The Crockett kids on Kellogg Street. From left: Walt, Carolyn, and me.

team. Looking back it really wasn't much of a tryout. Coach had us take some layups and foul shots and run wind sprints. I could shoot and made most of my shots. Nobody else did. Being a fourth-grader meant I didn't get much playing time, but I was thrilled because it was the only time I played on the same team with my older brother Walt.

We had a solid, if not deep, team my final year at Cathedral. The starters, myself included, played the entire game, unless we got into foul trouble. We beat every team except one. We couldn't beat St. Patrick's, which had Chris Jerome, the city's best player. Chris would go on to be an all-state player in high school and college. But in eighth grade he was still learning the game and struggled shooting. However, Chris was already nearly six feet tall, and a good five inches taller than our starting center. He would get the ball in the lane, throw it up, get the rebound, put it up again, get the rebound again, and eventually score. If they kept rebound statistics, he easily would have had twenty or so offensive rebounds every time we played. We almost beat St. Patrick's once. At our season-ending invitational tournament, we put in our back-up big man in to cover Chris. He was actually bigger and did a great job. Still, Chris matched my game-high twenty points and we lost again. I imagined teaming with Chris in high school. I didn't know that this would be my final game of school basketball. Ever.

I was also introduced to chess at Cathedral. It was in eighth grade and a classmates' dad, Mr. Holman, offered to teach anyone interested in the game. I liked board games, especially anything analytical, so I signed up immediately. We practiced for weeks culminating in a tournament. I finished runner-up and received a trophy with the king chess piece on top of a stand. It was different, and it was cool. Over the years all my trophies and awards have disappeared, except that one. For some reason, be it nostalgia or maybe because it wasn't a sports trophy, I hung on to it. It was probably around this time I realized that my smarts, not my athletic skills might just be the best way off the Hill.

Cathedral School not only shaped who I became as an adult; it also hardened me. Once in sixth grade, a fight broke out in the schoolyard, and like everybody else I bunched around the action. The consequence for fighting at school was the business end of the principal's paddle. I knew this because a year earlier I got into a fight and paid the price. This time I was shocked to get called into Sister Gerald's office with the two pugilists. Apparently, and I'll deny this to my grave, a teacher accused me of blocking and preventing her from breaking up the fight. Now, I was a bit chubby and maybe overzealous while checking out the schoolyard action, but her version made it sound like I was purposely boxing her out.

The afternoon of the fight the principal came to my classroom, called me to the front of the room, told me to bend over a desk, and then paddled me right in front of my peers. Sister Gerald was strong. It hurt and I cried. Corporal punishment at Cathedral was real. If it wasn't the paddle, it was a ruler to the knuckles and the threat to tell your mother. The latter was bad news for me, because Ma worshipped the nuns. They could do no wrong. If I upset them I paid the price again at home.

Despite that, I valued my education at Cathedral. It was challenging and the staff kept it enjoyable. In class we regularly played brain-teasing games and contests. I looked forward to the annual geography bee, and always fared well. The chief reason for this success was my siblings, especially Carolyn. We were a year apart and would quiz each other with maps to stay sharp. For example, I could name every state capital in elementary school. I recall a pop quiz in seventh-grade social studies class. Sister Elsa listed twenty states and asked us to write down the capitals. Of the fifteen or so kids in the class the average score was four. I nailed all twenty with the next highest being seven. Our class worked on capitals for two weeks; it was an easy two weeks for me.

During junior high school I started to notice girls. At one time or another I had a crush on every girl in my class. However, I was also afraid of every girl in my class and I rarely spoke to them. I wasn't ready for girls and figured it was better that way, but it shouldn't have been so hard. I was a good athlete, an excellent student, and I never caused trouble. You would think these were all likable qualities, but apparently not enough to be popular or part of the in-crowd. No question, more conversation and a little charm probably would have helped break the ice. I just couldn't talk to girls without becoming befuddled, and I didn't actually relax around them until college. The weeks before and after my eighth-grade graduation were telling. Three events transpired that had me wondering if things would ever get better.

We didn't have a yearbook or superlatives at Cathedral, but a list appeared just before graduation. I was told the girls were behind the list. It named five boys and five girls under the following categories: Best Looking, Most Athletic, Funniest, and Most Likely to Succeed. There were less than twenty boys in my grade, so I figured odds were good that I'd get recognized for something. When I saw the list my name appeared just once—Most Likely to Succeed. I didn't make the cut in any other category. Even though this was random and meaningless, I was hurt.

The day after graduation the prettiest girl in our class had a party, and I was invited. This was huge, since I'd never been invited to a party. A friend ran up to me on the eve of the party and told me that Katie, another classmate, wanted to hook up with me. Katie was beautiful and physically mature for an eighth-grader. I was attracted to her, so of course this news was paralyzing. I tried to get my friend to elaborate on what Katie meant by "hook up," but he just played with me; or maybe he didn't know, either. I was a wreck, literally sweating about this party and Katie. I arrived at the party fashionably late, since I didn't want to appear desperate. My buddy came rushing over.

"Eddie, did you hear about Katie?"

I tried to be cool. "No, what's up?"

Apparently the night before, Katie was playing stickball with friends and took a bat to the head. She was mostly fine, but had some swelling around one of her eyes. She would not be able to make the party. I was so relieved. It would be two years before I'd see Katie again.

Fourth of July celebrations always proved to be the biggest party of the year on Munjoy Hill. There were parades and sporting games played during the day. People all over The Hill hosted parties and then there were fireworks at night.

On one particular holiday in the mid-1970s, 60 Kellogg Street was a popular place, mainly due to one thing—drugs. An older brother regularly got high, primarily on marijuana, and invited friends to light up in his bedroom. I'd watch his buddies race upstairs, visit him for an hour or so, and then scurry out through a cloud of smoke. I was innocent and didn't pay much attention to what was going on. To his credit he never exposed me to the drugs. Funny, this was the only time I could say with a straight face that my house was a destination spot. I assumed the weed overpowered the other less desirable odors.

It was a beautiful sunny day and the family was relaxing on the front porch. I remember Ma, Grammy, and Grampa sitting for hours in folding chairs enjoying the sunshine and just watching all the people. Excitement was high, and then Walter came to ratchet it up even higher.

It was midafternoon and everyone was having a fine time. I was playing ball in the street when out of the corner of my eye I noticed somebody stumbling down Kellogg Street. It was my father. Walter showed up at the porch and, as always, an argument ensued. Grampa and my father exchanged heated words. By this point, I was a teenager and I got into the act. The scene grew uglier and uglier. The only way to get rid of Walter when he was in this condition was to call the police to come take him away. As this was going on, my brother was in his room getting stoned and oblivious to what was happening outside. Well, at least until he heard all the sirens. When the sirens started to ring through the neighborhood, he realized the cops were fast approaching. All the potheads in his room suddenly jumped to their feet and panicked thinking the cops were coming for them. The pot went flying, some guys stuffed it down their pants, and quickly tried to hide the paraphernalia. Meanwhile, downstairs, the cops were actually dragging away my father kicking and screaming. The police officers were great, very apologetic to Ma and her parents. The Portland Police Department knew our place well, of course—this wasn't their first visit to 60 Kellogg Street.

Chapter Seven
Cheverus

In June of 1975, I began working with my brother Jimmy, who was in his mid-20s, helping him make deliveries for Nappi's Bakery. At that age, Jimmy alternated between living in an apartment in Portland and at home. I was 13 and not old enough to get a work permit, but another set of hands was always appreciated. Most mornings Jimmy would pick me up at the crack of dawn and drive to the bakery. Once there, he'd check the orders and we'd load up the van.

The job was very physical. I'd imagined that since a loaf of bread or package of rolls was very light, moving the product around would be easy. Well, the products were stacked in trays and most accounts wanted multiple units. We had to use a dolly at most stops, and my primary job was to load the dolly. Since Jimmy was always in a hurry, I'd grab as many trays as I could handle and get them out the door. Lifting one tray at a time was frowned upon, because it took too long. I must admit it was a good workout for a kid too young to be officially on the clock. Jimmy took good care of me though. He paid me with egg rolls. Nappi's made the best egg rolls, a golden six-count, I've ever had. I'd eat them straight out of the bag for lunch. At the end of each day, Jimmy would square up the route and account for any goods I polished off. On sunny

My first real job was at George's Deli in Monument Square when I was 14.
Photo by Dr. Henry Pollard, courtesy of Jessica Pollard Lantos.

days, his boss would invite the drivers and their sidekicks, if any, to his home in North Deering to enjoy a dip in the pool after the long day. That was a cool fringe benefit.

One of Jimmy's best accounts was George's Delicatessen located in the heart of Monument Square. George's was owned by George Rosen and it was famous for its pastrami sandwiches. It was a Portland institution. The manager of George's was a young man named Tommy Jones. Tommy knew our family situation well, since his sister was good friends with my sister Carolyn.

One day in early July, Tommy noticed me helping Jimmy on the bread van and asked, "Would you like to be a busboy here?"

I was excited and quickly responded. "Yeah, when can I start?"

"How about tomorrow?"

I was on cloud nine! My first real job, and I would get paid cash for it. This was too good to be true. The deli was only a half-mile from my house, so I wouldn't even need transportation. Of course, there was a glitch: I wouldn't turn 14, and thus be eligible to work, for three more weeks. Once he realized my age, Tommy acknowledged that I needed a work permit to work at the restaurant.

Tommy could sense that I was bummed.

"Come to the deli on your birthday and you can start working."

I arrived bright and early on July 31 and continued working full-time until school started. Hiring me was a risky proposition for Tommy. The deli sat around the corner from Lincoln Park and the county jail, so the staff, primarily Tommy, regularly had to push away the bums, including my father, who came to George's daily begging for food scraps.

It didn't take long until I saw my father scrounging around outside the restaurant. Part of my busboy duties included emptying garbage into trash cans in the back alley. As I opened the door I heard Tommy talking to somebody. I immediately realized it was my father.

"Walter, you can't be out here during business hours. Come by before we open or after we close."

"I know, I know. Sorry. I saw food and figured it was OK."

"It's not OK. Come back when we close."

Walter scurried out of the alley. Tommy turned and saw me.

"What are you doing?"

"I was just taking out the trash. Do you know my father?"

"I do. I like him. But he's a very sick man."

"Sick? He's a drunk. Why are you helping him?"

"Because I know what being a drunk is. I'm an alcoholic. It's impossible to understand, I know. But, remember this. You don't have to be like that. Work hard and stay out of trouble."

Tommy paused. "Let's get back to work. We can talk later if you'd like. I'm sorry about that."

Tommy, indeed a recovering alcoholic himself, understood and protected me by keeping me focused. He made it clear that my life could be different. His thoughtfulness stayed with me forever.

Like most boys who attended Cathedral, including my brothers, the next stop was Cheverus High School. Cheverus was an all-boys Jesuit high school on Ocean Avenue, approximately three miles from Kellogg Street. I had three options to get to school. I could walk, hitchhike, or take a city bus. The school recommended the latter and provided a bus pass, so it didn't cost anything. I would hitchhike on the days I missed the bus. My closest bus stop was more than a half-mile away on Pearl Street, or more precisely, the west side of Lincoln Park.

Lincoln Park is a two-acre urban park in downtown Portland. Following the Great Fire of 1866, Lincoln Park was built as the city's first public common. Named in honor of recently assassinated President Abraham Lincoln, the green was originally a little wider. From east to west it spanned from Franklin Street to the Central Fire Station, only to get skinnier when the Arterial was constructed. The park's flat grassy terrain was dotted with trees and lined with wood-planked benches bolstered by concrete supports. A network of walking paths emanates from the centrally located Parisian fountain.

In my youth, Lincoln Park was infamous as a home for drunks and bums. This baffled me, since the Portland Police Department was at the southeast corner of the park. The authorities often appeared to be doing nothing about the activity. The grounds were not a safe place, but it's where high school students collected each weekday morning at seven to catch the school bus. On any given morning there would be masses of men, having spent the night sprawled on the benches or against the trees, bumming the professionals on their way to work or the kids waiting for the bus. On many occasions I would see the same guy on a bench at seven in the morning and three in the afternoon.

I attended Cheverus for two years, but I stopped taking the bus during freshman year. One of the bums always around the park was my father. I saw him often, sometimes in the morning as I walked down Congress Street or after I arrived at the park.

If Walter spotted me he kept his distance. We were both embarrassed. My luck finally ran out on an overcast morning in April 1976. I was waiting at the bus stop with dozens of classmates all decked out in our jackets and ties, when out of nowhere this bum stumbled into our circle with his hands extended begging for change.

It was my father.

"Any change? Come on, guys, anything you can spare?" asked Walter. "Hey, hey, I need smokes, can you help me out?"

An upperclassman chided him.

"Get lost! If I had any money I wouldn't give it to you anyway. You'd just spend it on more booze."

Another kid chimed in.

"Get outta here, you drunk. How about getting a job?"

Walter ignored these guys and moved closer to my circle of friends.

"Any change guys? Anything?

Suddenly he was looking right at me asking for change. And then I realized my father was so out of it that he didn't even recognize his own son while hitting him up for money. It was devastating. He was 42. He looked ancient with a long scraggly beard, mangy hair, and torn clothes. He couldn't have weighed 100 pounds soaking wet.

"Just a few bucks, that's all," he asked me.

The kids at the bus stop typically tried to ignore the bums, but the panhandling was constant and couldn't always be avoided. Some guys would give the drunks a hard time, pushing them out of the way and chastising them to "Get a life."

This was different. Some of the guys knew my situation, and worse, knew my father.

As Walter stood in our group everyone fell silent. It felt like everyone was looking at me.

I was mortified and I panicked. All I could think to do was run. So I did. I got as far as Washington Avenue, nearly a half-mile, before stopping to catch my breath. I paced trying to figure out what the hell had just happened. Was I more upset that he humiliated me or that he had no idea I existed? Do I hitchhike to school and face my bus-stop classmates there? No way. Do I run home and tell Ma? No. I skipped school for the only time ever. I wandered around Munjoy South and The Hill until it was time to go home.

I never caught the bus at Lincoln Park again.

Cheverus High was an excellent school, and the community was welcoming, but I was never comfortable there. To be fair, most of my discomfort was self-induced. I was insecure and bitter about the bad hand I'd been dealt. I defined myself as a welfare kid with a bum for a father, a down-and-out mother, and a pigsty for a home. I looked at my peers and felt inadequate. It was a private school, and many of my classmates came from nice homes in the suburbs, drove expensive cars, and walked around with pockets full of cash—at least that was my perception. I never expressed these feelings publicly or I probably wouldn't have had any friends.

I only stayed at the school for two years, but I did learn many valuable lessons that helped steer me through life. The most punishing lesson was getting cut from the freshman basketball team by a coach named Charlie Malia. Basketball was always my first athletic love, and I wanted more than anything to be on the freshman team. Coach Malia, (disrespectfully called "Yakka" behind his back) selected fifteen boys for the squad after two tryouts. I was encouraged about making the team since Malia had watched me score twenty against St. Patrick's. He knew I could play ball and I was clearly one of the top fifteen players. After tryouts, my name didn't appear on the "Made the Team" list posted outside his office.

I was crushed, but not shocked. I had tried out for football that fall and became the starting wide receiver and punter on the freshman team. Our team struggled, losing all six of its games. Our coach was determined to run the ball which proved frustrating to the team's split end, me. In our fourth game the coaches finally called a pass play. Surprised by the play call, I apparently ran the wrong route and the pass fell incomplete. The next game, with no heads up, I was replaced as wide receiver and punter and put in the line to block. Regrettably, I quit the team.

After school the following week, I was in the gym shooting hoops to get ready for basketball season. Malia, the new freshman basketball coach, who was direct and intimidating, saw me in the gym and asked, "What are you doing here, aren't you playing football?"

I told him I'd stopped playing and he jumped all over me.

"You quit? I don't want quitters on my basketball team."

It hurt, but I was still determined to make the team. I just figured he was trying to send me a message, and would be fair when evaluating me during tryouts. Silly me. I didn't know at the time there were other issues in play. Malia had a history with my family and my football follies gave him justification to stick it to me at tryouts.

Malia was a renowned cross country and track coach and he taught social studies. While I was at Cheverus, the cross country team was in the midst of winning more than one hundred consecutive regular season meets, and my brother Walt was one of the team's top runners. Before moving to Cheverus, Malia taught at Cathedral School and coached my brother Danny in basketball. While practicing in junior high, Danny had an altercation with Malia and delivered a right hand to his face. Not a bright move for a middle-schooler to hit his coach but, as we'd all learn later, maybe Yakka had it coming.

In high school, Danny became an All-State distance runner. Yet as fate would have it, his success would not be for the purple and gold of Cheverus, but for the blue and white of Portland High. Danny started high school at Cheverus, but Malia also moved from Cathedral to Cheverus when Danny was a freshman. I'm not saying Danny transferred to Portland following that first year because Yakka had arrived to coach cross country and track, but I doubt the timing was coincidental.

The freshman basketball tryouts were very competitive. The team was loaded. In 1975-76, freshmen were not allowed to play on varsity or junior varsity teams. As a result, sometimes freshmen teams were as good or even better than the JV teams. The freshman team that year dominated, winning every game easily. The team was talented, but not incredibly deep. The starters and next five off the bench could play, but the back end of the roster was filled with developing players and beginners. I would have been a strong candidate to come off the bench with this team. After being cut, I received many condolences from the guys who made it. I was upset. There was even one kid who couldn't dribble or even make a layup, but he got to play while I watched from the stands. In the grand scheme, Yakka made his point. I never quit anything again. He taught me a valuable lesson, and I hated him for it.

In the late 1970s, Portland was blessed with five outstanding high schools. The two public schools, Portland High and Deering High, were co-educational for grades 10-12. Catherine McAuley was an all-girls Catholic high school and Cheverus was an all-boys Jesuit high school. And Waynflete School, was a private co-ed college preparatory school located in the West End.

The public schools, of course, were free, while the private ones required tuition. The cost to attend Cheverus my first year was approximately seven hundred dollars. Seeing as Ma had no money, I qualified for a work-study program which served as an alternative to tuition. My job was to clean classrooms, basically empty the trash and wipe the chalkboards, after school every day. It took me about an hour. Since I played a sport every season I had a decision to make. Do I skip work-study and go to practice, or do my work-study job and not play sports? Fortunately I was supervised by two wonderful ladies who always covered for me. They were the best. They let me come in after practice and clean the classrooms. Honestly, I learned more about business and life through my work-study jobs than I did in the classroom.

During my first year I also answered phones at the Cheverus rectory. The phone didn't ring much, so I usually did my homework while sitting in the office. I was on duty one Saturday evening when my faith and trust in friendship was tested. Two longtime friends from my Cathedral days decided to test my loyalty. One friend gave me a call and started dissing the other friend. The mutual friend was actually sitting beside the caller listening to my responses, checking to see if I'd pile on to the insults. I didn't bite. Weeks later I learned of their "just having fun" call and was not pleased. I wondered, "Is this what friends do, and what friendship is all about?" I thought it was bullshit. It was crap like that, in addition to my father, which kept me guarded and unwilling to trust or believe in people for a long time.

While playing intramural basketball during my sophomore year my temper and poor sportsmanship got the better of me. After getting cut from the freshman team, despite loving the sport, I didn't pick up a basketball for more than a year. During my sophomore year I decided to pass on trying out for the JV and varsity teams. I always regretted that decision. I figured my bed was made and reluctantly let it go. But the itch to play came back when a few friends asked me to put together an intramural team. We called ourselves, Kett's Nets.

The team name came about because of my nickname. On the Hill, we created nicknames using the last syllables of a person's name. Everybody at school and on The Hill, where I was told the handles originated, called me D-Kett. The nickname was derived from the last syllable of my two names, Ed-die Croc-kett, thus D-Kett. Walt was called Ter-Kett, and I have to admit the last syllables of our names had a nice ring to them. The system was tried on everyone, but since ours rolled easily off the tongue, they stuck.

Kett's Nets played other teams made up of freshmen and sophomores. Our club was solid. I was a guard, so I recruited two big men, emphasizing girth and height. Rebounding was not a problem. Finding a couple more guard types was tougher. Since I was the primary ball handler and planned to carry the scoring load, I had to find a few steady role players. I wanted ballers who would play defense, and not commit turnovers. I found the perfect guys, and we dominated the first half of the season. Our only competition came from a team called Hayman's Heroes. They were an average team until a starter from the previous year's freshmen team opted not to play for the school and joined the Heroes. Red was a terrific player, six-feet, three-inches, very athletic and physical. We played twice and both times he locked me down pretty good. The Heroes edged us for the championship. I didn't handle losing well. With every turnover, missed shot, or defensive lapse, I would express my displeasure and hang my head. During one game, I even started mouthing off to the student referee. The ref, Mark, who was a guard on the varsity team, finally had had enough. When the game ended he grabbed my shirt, threw me up against the wall, and gave me a good tongue-lashing. I don't remember exactly what he said, but he scared the shit out of me and he got into my head. In his defense, my behavior was out of line and needed to be addressed. Mark turned a light on for me that day. I immediately shaped up and became a better teammate, and going forward a better person.

After my sophomore year, I had every intention of returning to Cheverus. I was once again offered a work-study job on the summer paint crew to cover the new nine hundred dollar tuition. I declined the offer and wrote a letter to the school president asking Cheverus to waive tuition. I'm not sure what compelled me to ask for the waiver, other than recognizing I didn't have the money. I didn't think I had anything to lose. I certainly didn't want to do the summer work-study again. Working forty plus hours a week with nothing to show for it, other than tuition being waived, was maddening. Of course, I did the math. Ten weeks or four hundred hours to cover the nine hundred dollar tuition came out to $2.25 per hour. The minimum wage in 1977 was $2.30 per hour. Honestly I looked at it as cheap labor and I wasn't willing to do it again. Interestingly, Walt had been assigned work-study all four years at Cheverus and totally blew it off, and he got away with it. Then again he was a state champion distance runner on a team with a one hundred-meet winning streak and a coach, Charlie Malia, who appeared to get whatever he wanted. Do you think he was going to send his best runner packing because he blew off work-study? No bleeping way.

During his time at Cheverus, Walt was undisciplined and didn't apply himself. I don't recall him ever bringing a book home, and his grades reflected it. Although Walt was incredibly bright, he didn't try and was in danger of not graduating. Finally, Walt was told late in his senior year that if he didn't ace fourth-quarter marine biology, he would not graduate. I was disappointed that the Cheverus administration let him slide for three and a half years before holding him accountable academically. Since Walt had flunked the first three quarters of marine biology, completely his fault, he had to get an A in the fourth quarter or fail the class. I know this sounds cynical, but I found the timing interesting. Walt pulled crap like this for years and was forgiven. The adults there turned a blind eye and let him skate through. However, by the spring, Cheverus and Charlie Malia didn't need his running skills anymore, so their recourse was to threaten his graduation status. To this day, Cheverus is accused of recruiting talented athletes. They didn't recruit my brother, but they did something even worse: They used him for sport. Fortunately, Walt got off his ass and produced an A in the fourth quarter to narrowly pass marine biology, and graduate on time. It should not have come down to that.

Anyway, even though I turned to cross country and track after my football and basketball episodes, unlike Walt, I was not a good runner. Therefore, I pegged my tuition waiver hopes on good grades and hoped for mercy. I was a hard-working honor student and thought maybe that would resonate. I pointed all this out in my letter, dropped it in the mail, and anxiously awaited a response.

The Cheverus president responded promptly to my letter. He was brief and direct. He complimented my success at the school and offered to waive half the tuition. I would need to pay the balance if I wanted to return for my junior year. I thought the offer was fair, especially since I didn't expect anything, but it made my decision more difficult. I had worked all summer as a camp counselor at the YWCA, and had banked just over five hundred dollars. During the summer of 1977 the city provided jobs to low-income kids. Walt, Carolyn, and I took advantage of the offer and hurried down to Portland High School to sign up. I applied for the camp counselor position and got it. While filling out the paperwork in the Portland High library I glanced to my left and saw a young, pregnant girl doing the same thing. We made eye contact and much to my surprise it was my Cathedral classmate, Katie. We said our hellos and went our separate ways, never seeing each other again. I suddenly realized what "hook up" in eighth grade could have meant.

The decision about where to go to school was exclusively mine. Do I take my savings and go back to Cheverus or transfer to Portland? There wasn't any additional money available at home. Ma didn't have two nickels to rub together, and my father was still spending his nights in Lincoln Park (I saw him passed out on the park benches as I made my way to and from the YWCA). Although at times I was uncomfortable at Cheverus, I genuinely liked the school and the guys were great. Ultimately the decision to transfer came down to two things. First, with Walt graduating, the expectation that I had to go to Cheverus was eased a bit (of course, Danny had transferred to Portland years earlier, so there was precedence). The biggest reason was that I didn't want to part with my life savings. That might sound ridiculous, but five hundred dollars to me in 1977 was a lot of money. Having never had any money, I was an instant saver. I opted to keep the money for the future, hopefully for college. Still, I put off the decision until two days before school started. All along, Ma thought I was going back to Cheverus, having weighed the pros and cons of transferring and having secured the $450 to cover tuition.

My biggest fear about attending Portland High School was that I didn't know anyone. Most of Portland's student body came from the public schools, so I'd essentially be starting over as a junior. I finally found the nerve to leave the house, make the trek down Congress Street, walk into Portland High, and enroll. Since classes were starting in two days, the administration wasn't expecting me. I walked into the main office and announced to the secretary that I wanted to come to Portland High. She directed me to a counselor who sat me down and asked a lot of questions.

"Who are you? Where do you live? Where did you go to school?"

Once they learned that I was a junior in good standing coming from a local school the grilling got softer. We were talking about classes when the enrollment process hit a snag. I explained that I was an honors student at Cheverus, and would like to enroll in all the junior year honors level courses. My last-minute decision was going to bite me in the ass. With school starting in just forty-eight hours I was informed that all the honors classes required recommendations. It wasn't that they didn't believe what I told them about my grades (although I didn't have my transcript in tow), they just weren't going to blindly take my word for it. The result of my unscheduled visit to Portland High was I got enrolled, but my class schedule was soft. For example, I had aced Algebra I and Geometry Honors at Cheverus and was scheduled to take Algebra II honors, but due to no transcript or teacher recommendation I was placed in a mid-level Algebra II class. The counselor was not able to get me into any honors courses. Clueless, and not understanding the impact that course selection had on college admittance, I happily accepted my new schedule.

This is me in high school, sporting a "Nowhere Else But 'Portland'" T-shirt.

Chapter Eight
Portland High School

Portland High School was established in 1821, making it one of the oldest high schools in the nation. In 1863, the school moved to its current location on Cumberland Avenue. The physical size of the school, which in effect took up a whole city block, was prodigious. I was moving from a school of approximately three hundred boys in four grades to a co-ed public high school with more than 1,500 students in just three grades. The junior class alone was bigger than all of Cathedral and Cheverus combined. I found it overwhelming at first, and might have reconsidered the transfer if not for cross-country. After getting cut from the basketball team at Cheverus, I grudgingly turned my attention to the family sport, for the boys anyway, distance running. I ran cross-country and indoor track my sophomore year at Cheverus, and had a good time, mainly cheering on Walt's excellence. Walt finished third in the state in cross-country and was the state champion in the indoor two-mile. He was the athlete in the family. I on the other hand jokingly referred to myself as an athletic supporter.

In elementary school, Sister Conrad pulled me aside after observing me run and gasped, "What's that? You're galloping, not running." Apparently I had a hitch in my stride. The following sums up my high school running career. I had the distinction of finishing in last place in at least one race every year of high school. As a freshman and sophomore it was commonplace, but as a junior, and even as a senior when I was competitive, I still managed to finish last at least once.

I joined the Portland cross-country team at practice following the first day of school and immediately began to get comfortable. Of all the teams I've ever been on, this one was my favorite. Partly due to unrealistic expectations, my reception was incredibly warm. The team was good, but not talented enough to challenge the top clubs. They surmised that getting the younger brother of two state champions was a real coup. "He must be pretty good, right?" was the expectation.

Although I was sorry to disappoint, the team still welcomed me with open arms. The coach, Mr. Bogdanovich, was terrific. Danny had been a captain on his 1971 state champion team, and Mr. Bog, as everyone called him, knew me from his days manning the Portland Exposition Building door on Park Avenue at wrestling events in the early 1970s. Wrestling, which in those days featured the likes of Chief Jay Strongbow, the Valiant Brothers, George "the Animal" Steele, and others, was a hot ticket in Portland. The traveling show came to town on a biweekly basis during its heyday (before it exploded in popularity with WrestleMania) and filled the Expo. Mr. Bog told Danny to send his little brothers down and he'd let us in, no charge. Walt and I were regular attendees at these wrestling matches and we appreciated his kindness. We'd see these characters on Saturday television and then get to see them live at the Expo. Yes, I knew it was fake, but it was also a blast. Mr. Bog was a class act. I felt right at home with this team.

It sounds crazy to think I didn't know anybody at Portland High School after living in Portland my whole life, but I was shy as a youngster, both at school and in the neighborhood, and most of the kids I played with in elementary and junior high went to the parochial high schools. The few who did go to public school after Cathedral either weren't close friends or never made it to Portland High. I was indeed a fish out of water, and one incident during the first week left me doubting my decision to transfer. When Walt was in grade school he went on a class trip to the animal farm in Gray. At some point he was swimming with the fishes in the exhibit. Not sure if he got pushed in or was dared, but the end result was a nickname—Fish. So, since I was the little brother, his peers started calling me Little Fish. I'm like, "What the fuck? I didn't jump in with the fishes, leave me the hell alone."

Fortunately, the moniker lost its appeal by high school. D-Kett took over and I had forgotten about it until the first week at Portland High. As I walked through the crowded halls trying to get to my next class, I heard somebody yell, "Hey, Little Fish." Although I didn't acknowledge it, I turned a deep shade of red before whirling out of sight. To make it worse, from my perspective anyway, the dis came from two extremely popular classmates who didn't even know me. Thankfully "Little Fish" never came up again, but for two years I treaded lightly around those two.

The cross-country team was a safe haven. The team was senior laden, but had a trio of talented underclassmen. Fellow juniors Mike Whitlock and Bill Cooper were consistent scorers, and sophomore newcomer Tony Esposito was arguably the best of the lot. The guys realized immediately that I wasn't much help to them on the trails. However, we got along great both on and off the course. In my comfort zone, I was personable with a sly sense of humor. We'd laugh it up logging mile after mile in training. Later, we'd occasionally get together and have some beers. I had made it sixteen and a half years without ever committing the great "sin" of taking a drink. My mother successfully instilled in me the fear that if I did, I would be just like my father. Until this point, I had removed myself from most social gatherings. I was ready to get out there and have some fun.

One Saturday night Coop and two senior teammates picked me up around six for a night of carousing. The plan was to have a few beers and then go to a party in the West End. I was pumped about the party, because my sister Carolyn was going to be there. Carolyn was a senior in high school, and someone I considered a party master who had never hung out with her little brother. We were both looking forward to whooping it up, but I never made it. My senior friends bought six-packs of Colt 45s and bottles of Old Duke at the package store. I had no idea what I was doing and threw down three Colt 45s and some wine. For a while I was a very happy camper, but as we made our way to the party I was hanging out the car window puking my guts out. It was so bad my friends took me home. They went to the party. Coop told Carolyn about my evening. I'm sure she was disappointed and chuckling at the same time.

While the downside of attending Portland High was not knowing anyone, the upside was that it provided me with the opportunity to make new friends—and to see girls in the classroom again. I didn't muster the courage to actually ask a girl on a date until late in my senior year. As a 16-year-old junior, my hormones were raging, and girls looked even better than they did when I was a pre-teen. I was definitely *ready* to date, but didn't know *how* to go about it. Sitting directly behind me in math class was a lovely girl named Diana. I had a huge crush on her. The issue was that she always had a boyfriend. I took that as "not available." Probably a commandment thing; "Thanks, Mom!"

I was surrounded by beautiful girls in this class. Sitting beside me was Peggy. I went the entire year without ever saying a word to Peggy. I really wanted to say something, but I didn't have the nerve. One day she dropped her pencil and it rolled under my desk. I picked it up and gave it back to her, but I could only produce an embarrassed smile—pitiful. If I had more confidence, I had plenty of time in that class to flirt with girls, since I was bored and unchallenged. I should have been in the Algebra II honors class, and apparently my attitude showed it. Our teacher wasn't a fan. At the end of the year, we had a final exam that was scheduled to take the entire class period. When I finished the test I walked up to her desk to pass it in. She jumped all over me with, "Get back to your seat and check your work." Her eyebrows burrowed deep into her dark-rimmed glasses.

I bowed my head and scurried back to my seat dreadfully confused. I had already checked my work and didn't understand why she was so upset. Allegedly, she thought I was showing off and being disrespectful. Only fifteen minutes had transpired when I attempted to hand in the test. That pissed her off. Following her tongue-lashing, I sat timidly twiddling my thumbs waiting for someone else to hand in their test so I could, too. It felt like forever.

My brother Danny Paul, who was born in 1953 and was in his early-20s at the time, would soon graduate from the University of Maine at Farmington (and would later earn his master's degree from Middlebury College). Danny was doing his student teaching at Portland High School in the spring of 1978 and was assigned to my English class. I didn't talk to him in class, but he was living at home and I asked questions and sought extra help there. That was much easier than asking questions in class with other students around. It was also cool that my classmates didn't know he was my brother. Naturally, different last names threw them off. The afore-mentioned Diana from algebra class was also in the English class and found out we were brothers. I was home one evening when out of the blue Danny asked me, "What's wrong with you?"

"What are you talking about?"

He told me Diana had been asking about me. I said nothing. He just gave me the "you-are-a-dumbass" look. Predictably, I did nothing with this information.

It turns out the girl who would later become the true love of my life was in my chemistry class. Martha Rand was beautiful, smart, and popular. She was an outstanding athlete and a top tennis player. She was great at a lot of other sports, but opted for cheer-leading over soccer, field hockey, or basketball in high school, since that was the thing to do in those days. She was not the most ded-icated student. I remember watching Martha sit in the back cor-ner of chemistry class with her feet up on the windowsill socializing with Peggy and other friends. Meanwhile, I was in the front row taking notes, talking to nobody. We only spoke to each other once that year and only by happenstance. She was leaving the classroom just as I was trying to get back in. The door was not very wide, and our shoulders brushed. Turning my head away I said, "Excuse me," and kept going.

That's it. I can't tell you if she responded, since I was red-faced and moving fast.

High school wasn't a total loss with girls. I took a journal-ism class my junior year and was assigned to work on the newspa-per and yearbook. This led to being the sports editor of the year-book my senior year. While staying after school selecting pictures and crafting stories I became friendly with a classmate who was also on the staff, and I finally worked up the courage to ask her out. We dated for a few months and we went to the prom together. My time at Portland began with my first drink of alcohol and ended with my first kiss. It was an education.

During the summer after my junior year, I fully committed to running. As an incentive, I made a ridiculous one-sided bet with my brother Jimmy. I told him, "I'll run fifty straight days this summer, five miles or more, and if I fail, I'll give you five hundred dollars. If I do it, just pat me on the back and say congratulations." He immediately took the bet. He was always a smart one.

I knew I needed to improve to make varsity. Our team was solid, so I figured the bet would keep me motivated and committed—I still hated to lose, plus I was cheap. If I wouldn't give Cheverus five hundred dollars, damned if I'd hand Jimmy five bills without a fight. As a junior I was a top junior varsity runner, which meant there were ten runners ahead of me on varsity. Since four of them were seniors, the odds were good that I'd move up to varsity for my senior season. My goal was to be in the top seven seeing as only seven harriers ran in the big meets. With two former state champions in the house I had plenty of support. Surprisingly the person who was most helpful in my training was my brother David. David, the oldest of my mother's children, was born in 1945, making him sixteen years older than me. He joined the U.S. Coast Guard right out of high school and later worked with New England Telephone. He didn't run as a kid, but had recently taken up the sport as an adult. He joined the local track club and began organizing and directing numerous road races. David, who was in his 30s, became knowledgeable very quickly about everything related to running. He actually put together my workouts that summer.

Although the bet was silly, it was just what the doctor ordered. I ran outdoor track the previous spring and struggled to break five minutes in the mile. The better cross-country runners were running

This is me in Ma's kitchen, sporting my prom tux in the spring of 1979.

sub-five-minute miles for three miles, so I had to get busy. I needed more miles and serious speed work and in a hurry. I trusted that running a minimum of five miles a day with interval training thrown in would provide me with the mileage base and speed necessary to be competitive. When I arrived at cross-country practice in late August, it only took two minutes before realizing all the training was necessary. Thanks to the addition of two newcomers, the team was loaded. It was clear gaining a spot in the top seven was not guaranteed. On paper, based on all the returnees and the newcomers, I was on the outside looking in. But because I ran over three hundred miles that summer, I was comfortably in the top seven.

In the preseason our team wasn't considered championship material. But, much to our surprise and the league's, we would be crowned state champions that fall. Throughout the 1970s, Portland High dominated in track, but in cross-country we were always chasing Cheverus or South Portland or Lawrence. Portland had won its one and only cross-country title in 1971 (Danny's team), so our aspirations were more about being competitive, not champions. We gathered that something special was brewing at our first meet, a quad-meet at Saco's Thornton Academy where the first six runners across the finish line were all Portland Bulldogs. Espo won the race followed by Whit and Coop. I was the sixth man, coming in behind our two newcomers, Glen and Matt. It was obvious that we were talented and deep. Our top six were staunch.

After the race I overheard the Thornton coach say to Mr. Bog, "I think we just saw the state champions today." The team was pumped. I was relieved that the long summer spent building endurance had paid off. I loved these guys. The upperclassmen remain lifelong friends, tough, competitive, hard-working, fun-loving guys.

On training runs with my teammates, I'd see Walter on the streets or in Deering Oaks, but never go close enough to interact. We hadn't been face to face since the Lincoln Park bus stop fiasco when I was a freshman. Honestly, I expected to just get a call one day telling me my father was dead. And I didn't expect to show any emotion upon hearing the news. His passing would be sad, but a relief to me, heck to everyone, or so I reasoned. Our cross-country course ran two loops through Deering Oaks and we trained there nearly every day. The only saving grace was that my Portland teammates had no idea the drunk sprawled out on the sidewalk was my father. That was my secret and I kept it close.

Unknowingly, we were a great fit for our talented new teammates. In cross-country, the first five finishers count in scoring (your place counts toward the final tally), with the low cumulative total winning. We needed the new guys to compete if we were to challenge the top teams. We welcomed Glen and Matt with open arms and dared them to kick our asses. They made us better; after all, none of us wanted to get beat by the newcomers. Espo and Whit, our top two runners, led by example. Coop and I were more vocal leaders. Of course, Glen and Matt got my attention quickly by beating me in that first meet. Quietly I felt our team could be great if these two could keep it up.

Matt and Glen were two very different young men with secrets. They were rivals in middle school, and their personalities were night and day. Getting a word out of the shy and studious Matt was next to impossible. I liked him immediately, and made it my job to make him comfortable. I know Matt appreciated my attempts at humor and inclusion, even if he wasn't totally at ease. I only know this because a mutual friend told me so later that year. Matt also had a secret. He was gay. In 1978, that secret usually stayed locked in the closet. He came out as an adult, a move he didn't want to risk as a 16-year-old. There was no reason for Matt to share this with me, or anybody else, and I certainly didn't suspect it. I'd like to think I would have understood if he'd ever wanted to talk about it.

Glen also had a secret, a painful one. He was a talented athlete, not only an accomplished runner but a good basketball player. He was funny and outgoing—a joy to be around. Like Matt, he wanted this team to attain greatness. Glen and I talked daily. He was inquisitive, particularly about my Cheverus experience. He frequently asked me about my experiences with Coach Charlie Malia. I would learn why two decades later. Glen, like many other boys, was molested by Charlie Malia. The coach, who grew up on Munjoy Hill, may have cut me from a basketball team, but that was a minor infraction compared to the hurt and pain he caused the young victims he molested while a respected coach at Cheverus

High School. I learned about it in a news story that appeared in the *Portland Press Herald* twenty years later under the headline "Admitted Serial Molester at Cheverus." I would learn of others as well as the news rolled out and investigations continued.

The news story ran in 2000, but issues had been public since 1997, when a former student told a Cheverus official that Malia had sexually abused him. Malia denied the allegation, but agreed to quietly resign after finishing the school year. More allegations against Malia, both when he was at Cathedral Junior High School and at Cheverus High School in the 1960s and 1970s, followed. Students said the sexual abuse occurred in the school's locker room, at Malia's Portland apartment, and other places. The allegations included Malia grabbing a boy's genitals in a school shower, fondling a boy's genitals during a massage after a track workout, and masturbating another boy during visits to the boy's house. The victims said they feared Malia's power and authority, and did not try to report the incidents.

Glen was molested by Malia at age 14 while attending a running camp at Cheverus. Although I was not working at the camp, Walt was there. Glen took a liking to Walt right away, and had his heart set on attending Cheverus. A problem for Glen, as it was for us, was that he came from meager means and couldn't afford private school unless he received financial assistance. His running talent was his ticket to Cheverus. Glen was the most promising runner in his class, and he would have been a prime catch for Malia and his running dynasty. That dream was shattered following a hard workout at camp. Malia used to rub down his runners after workouts. He called Glen into the massage room and closed the door. Glen said the rubdown started out innocently enough, but before he realized what was going on Malia's hands were on his buttocks and moving toward his genitals. The stunned teenager froze before suddenly jumping off the table and racing out the door. Glen came back to camp the next day, avoided Malia, and finished the training.

Two years later, I'd transferred to Portland High and was running cross-country. Glen, following his camp experience, crossed Cheverus off his wish list and enrolled at Portland. He was an outstanding runner and a welcome addition to our squad. Glen never revealed what was really on his mind when he kept asking me about Coach Malia probably for the same reason he didn't say anything at the camp. I didn't pick up on his secret. He was a great kid, living with the burden of being molested by a trusted coach and did not have the courage or support to get it off his chest until he was a grown man in his late 30s. After the news broke, Cheverus High did one thing right—it removed Malia's name from its new outdoor track facility and washed its hands of the tormenter. Malia was never officially charged because too much time had passed since the abuse.

In one way, the Crockett boys were lucky. Whether it was the memory of Danny landing that right hand to his face years earlier, or the fact that we had two other feisty older brothers, Malia knew better than to mess with Walt or me. Thank God for the Pauls, because without them Walt and I would have likely been prime targets to a predator like him.

When our team actually won the state championship, it was a bittersweet day for me. A few days before the meet my grandfather, Howard Sterling Mayberry, was rushed to the hospital. At four in the morning on race day our phone rang and medical staff notified us that Grampa had passed away. It had been a long couple of days for the family. Everyone was on edge and working on little sleep.

Four hours later, I walked to the Expo for the bus ride to the state championship meet. The meet was at the Riverside Golf Course in Portland, so we didn't have far to travel. My heart was elsewhere, and I chose not to share the news with Mr. Bog or my teammates. We had a championship to claim, and I wasn't looking to be a downer. I felt good early in the race. I was near the front and suddenly realized I'd gone out too fast. About a mile in I began to labor both mentally and physically, and started to drop back. Much to my surprise, our usual number three runner, Coop, came up on my shoulder and nodded. I looked at him and huffed: "You have to get going!" After a few strides and no burst from Coop, I said, "Let's go," and proceeded to do a quarter-mile pick-up.

Thankfully Coop followed me, and more decisively kept going as I faded. Coop finished in the top twenty, and we beat South Portland and Lawrence by four points to win the state championship. Lawrence was stacked with four guys finishing in the top dozen. But, their fifth man finished eight spots behind me. Although I wasn't a scorer that day, I would playfully remind my teammates that if I'd run for the other Bulldogs (Lawrence High), we'd have been an also-ran again.

It was during my senior year of high school that I took a job at the Li'l Peach convenience store on Congress Street, directly across the street from The Corner. A dear friend, Charlie DiFazio, was working there and told me the owner was looking for help. Since Charlie recommended me, the owner hired me on the spot. The job was pretty basic, run the register and stock the shelves. The work was easy, but The Corner created lots of problems.

Although The Corner was devoid of activity most mornings, there was plenty of action with cars coming and going in the Li'l Peach lot. This confused me since there weren't any customers in

My Portland High School yearbook photo.

the store. It didn't take long before I caught on to what was happening. Morning was prime time for buying and selling drugs. There were many dealers on the Hill, and a plethora of wannabes in waiting. Transactions were taking place within feet of the front door. While waiting for customers I'd peer out the window and watch the traffic or trafficking outside. It was constant. Occasionally a police car would slowly drive by, but rarely stop. Maybe they thought business was good. I believe it was for some.

In the 1970s and early 1980s, The Corner was where idle Munjoy Hill ruffians, mainly guys, would hang out. They would start congregating as early as eight in the morning and not leave until well after midnight. I watched the goings-on up close while working at the Li'l Peach. I recall former classmates and friends coming into the store, looking me in the eyes, telling me to turn away, so that they could steal stuff (mostly beer and smokes). One night as I was closing up I walked into the cooler and found a former Little League teammate sitting there downing beers. He would have been content to stay in the cooler all night. After a few contentious minutes, he finally rose up and left the store, but not before stuffing a twelve-pack under his arm on the way out. This was a sign of things to come. A few years later he overdosed and died on the streets of Munjoy Hill.

I often worked alone, opening and closing the store on a regular basis. I wondered why the owner let me, just a teenager, handle that responsibility given what was happening around the store, but I think he just didn't want anything to do with it. He told me it was better to have somebody working in the store that the kids knew, and probably wouldn't mess with, than somebody who might protest and possibly get hurt. Still, I watched many of my peers sell drugs, drink excessively, and get arrested. Young people were dying, a few right on The Corner. It was bad.

We were increasingly worried about my brother Walt. Walt was a mini-Walter and everybody feared he'd follow his old man's path. Time and again I'd watch Walt leave work and mosey across the street to The Corner. Like Walter, Walt was personable and charming, and loved the streets. After he graduated from high school, Walt spiraled out of control. With no prospects for college, Walt settled into life on The Hill. He secured a job at the Community Center, which was perfect considering his outgoing personality and penchant for playing games. He could crawl out of bed fifteen minutes before his shift, throw on some sweats, and walk the two hundred yards to the Community Center. At work he played pool, cards, and shot hoops, while across the street his best buds, Teddy and David, waited for him. It was no surprise that when Walt punched out from work, he went over to join them.

Walt's routine became predictable. He joined his friends after work and partied all night, often never coming home. When he did make it home, he set his alarm to leave himself just enough time to bathe and get to work on time. He was always hungover. Walt would dawdle on The Corner until the well went dry, then move around The Hill. It was a few hours at the Bunker, George's Tavern, or the Stardust strip joint before eventually landing at the AMVETS. AMVETS was Walt's favorite spot. It was located on Washington Avenue and catered to a sketchy crowd. It offered cheap drinks and plenty of finger food, making it an affordable spot for a young adult with little money.

It was at AMVETS that he met Duncan.

Duncan was a seedy character and a prominent bookie, who preferred the company of young men to women. He was an older man and he preyed on them. Many desperate young men fell into his debt. Sadly, Walt was one of them. If a kid needed money or drugs Duncan would provide it, but at a cost. That debt was to be paid with sex. Duncan would feed them, clothe them, and provide whatever vice they needed in exchange for sexual favors. If a kid was down on his luck with the horses or sports teams, a blow job might wipe the slate clean. We all knew the stories. Walt denied doing any sexual favors for Duncan, and I believed him. We were a big family and our three older brothers would have kicked this guy's ass if he tried anything, and he knew it.

Walt liked the ladies, and was often successful at charming their pants off. One night in a drunken stupor at AMVETS he went home with an older woman (we'd call her a cougar today). By chance, she happened to live only a few houses down on Kellogg Street. It would be a one-night stand that lasted forever. Ma was not totally surprised when many years later this lady came calling on her for child support. Yes, unknown to Walt for a long time, his young lifestyle had produced a child and given Ma another granddaughter.

Walt was out of control and intervention was needed.

One weekend my older siblings waited for Walt to come home. They sat him down for a "come to Jesus" talk. They made it clear he had to get out of town, away from The Corner and away from Duncan and others like him, or he would end up on the streets like his father, or maybe even dead.

During this time, Ma was at her wits' end. She saw the cycle repeating. She knew something had to give. Ironically, the best option appeared to be the same one our father took, the military. Ma was not supportive of this option, and she laid some heavy guilt onto my older siblings.

She told them, "If he gets hurt or killed, it is on you." My mom knew how to lay on the serious guilt.

Nevertheless, Walt joined the Army in 1979. He was 20.

He did me a big favor before he left. He shared with me some of his escapades from around the neighborhood. At this time in his life, Walt was directionless. He spent too much time in the local bars, including a dive bar on India Street called Sangillo's. It may not be fair to characterize Sangillo's as a dive, but the place was scary from the outside. It sat on the corner of India and Fore streets just below Munjoy Hill, and the only window was on the front door. I vaguely recall bars on it. However, it was three blocks from the house and drinks were cheap. One evening Walt was in the bar shooting his mouth off when a fellow patron, bigger than Walt, had had enough and pulled a knife. Walt nearly shit his pants. He wasn't a fighter, but he'd drink you under the table and then talk smack about it. Like most cocky kids, he could be annoying. Walt was unarmed and backing off when out of nowhere another guy jumped in between the two, and got in the face of the knife wielder. Before Walt knew what was happening, his nemesis walked away leaving him facing this new adversary. This guy was much smaller than Walt, going about five-foot, eight-inches tall and maybe 150 pounds. The stranger looked Walt in the eyes and said, "Nobody messes with my cousin," and broke out into a huge smile.

Jimma Campbell, or Weasel as he was nicknamed, was the oldest son of my father's sister, Peggy. I knew Aunt Peggy, but only in passing. She and her six children lived in Kennedy Park. My father was close to the Campbells, but since we had nothing to do with him and the Campbells went to public schoo,l our paths rarely crossed.

Walt believed Weasel probably saved his life. The guy had blood in his eyes and knife fights at Sangillo's were not uncommon.

I valued this story, because it affected my behavior both immediately and going forward. I stayed away from places like Sangillo's. I had a big mouth, too, and I couldn't count on Jimma or his younger brothers to save my ass. This story and the danger associated with that lifestyle never left me. I wouldn't totally understand it for years, but it reminded me that blood is thicker than alcohol.

I am not looking to disparage my brother. Beyond my wife and children, there is not a person on this Earth I am more proud of than Walt. He turned his life around and became a husband, father, grandfather, and successful businessman.

Chapter Nine
A Guardian Angel

In the fall of 1978, Walter once again lay on the street near death. A priest came to administer Last Rites for an astonishing fifth time.

For the third time in eleven years, the cause of Walter's state could be tied to the Boston Red Sox. The first time happened after the Sox lost the World Series to the St. Louis Cardinals in 1967 and then it happened again in 1975 when they lost to the Cincinnati Reds in arguably the greatest World Series ever. Both were agonizing and proved more than Walter could handle. In 1975, the resurgent Boston Red Sox were led by two incredible rookies Fred Lynn and Jim Rice. By now, although Carl Yastrzemski was still on the roster, Jim Rice had become my favorite player. Early in his career he was often referred to as Jim Ed Rice. We shared the same middle name, so that probably won me over. Unfortunately, the Red Sox would have to beat the Big Red Machine without Rice, who broke his hand late in the season. The Red Sox fought back to square the series at three games apiece on Carlton Fisk's hand-waving home run off the left field foul pole, only to lose game 7, again, and go home empty-handed. In the aftermath, Walter was so distraught he drank himself into oblivion and was administered Last Rites for the fourth time.

117

The Red Sox struck again in 1978. In 1978, the Sox led the Yankees by 14 games, but managed to blow their lead and trailed the Yankees going into the last game of the season. On that final Sunday, the Red Sox beat the Toronto Blue Jays, while the Yankees lost to the Cleveland Indians, forcing a one-game playoff for the Division crown at Fenway Park. Both teams finished the season with identical records of 99–63.

The next day, in a tie-breaker game played at Fenway Park, the Yankees beat the Red Sox, 5–4. "Bucky Fucking Dent" is still a catchphrase that rings loudly and painfully in the ears of all Red Sox fans. The Yankee shortstop, who was a Punch and Judy hitter, lifted a soft flyball toward the Green Monster just clearing the wall to win the playoff game. It is 315 feet down the left field line in Fenway Park and this "shot" would not have traveled more than 330 feet if the wall hadn't been in the way.

It was devastating. The Red Sox lost and Walter immediately went on a bender. He was found unconscious and barely alive in Deering Oaks and it was assumed as it had been four previous times that death was imminent. A priest was called and he administered Last Rites, which in the Catholic Church is a sacrament meant to cleanse a person of his sins before they leave Earth and to protect them on their journey to the afterlife. Once again, despite all signs to the contrary and maybe because his sins were too numerous to be cleansed by a mere priest, Walter was not ready to take that journey. Instead, he found something entirely different and even more powerful—a guardian angel.

He was shipped to Togus Veterans Hospital in Augusta. Although he didn't die, his situation seemed more dire than ever. By all accounts, this stay truly represented his last chance for recovery.

The staff at Togus placed Walter in a padded cell and left him alone for a week to work through the horrors that always came with his plight. When the horrors ended, he remained bedridden for another three weeks to regain his strength.

While Walter was struggling to recover, his guardian angel appeared—Ann. Ann was a psychology intern at Togus, which proved to be a fascinating place to study the human mind. The brave soldiers who came through the doors at Togus were often damaged goods, and for those also trying to overcome an addiction to alcohol the road was not only difficult, but impossible for some.

So, Ann was given the unenviable task of trying to get Walter back on his feet and out the door as quickly as possible. Walter, however, had other ideas. He took a shine to Ann and used his best cons to remain in her care. Apparently, he looked even worse than he felt. At some point, he was well enough to be released, but he feigned a lingering sickness in order to stay put and close to Ann. During his recovery, he talked to her about life, dreams, and Alcoholics Anonymous.

For some reason, Ann saw something special inside this flawed and broken man. She could not share her feelings; that would have been unprofessional and, quite frankly, crazy. Yet somehow this five-time near-death loser, who had spent most of his last seventeen years drunk and homeless, successfully got inside her head.

Ann looked inside him and for some reason imagined she could save his lost soul.

As Walter was leaving Togus, he boldly asked Ann for her phone number.

She gave it to him.

Chapter Ten
University of Maine

Iapplied to three schools and two of them rejected me. Notre Dame and Connecticut said, "No thanks." The University of Maine at Orono accepted me, and I was relieved. I didn't visit any of the schools before I applied. I was somewhat familiar with Notre Dame and Connecticut from watching football and basketball games on television. I didn't know anything about the University of Maine except what was in the campus literature distributed at my high school. If Notre Dame or Connecticut had said, "yes," it would have been nice, but I couldn't have attended. Ma didn't have any money, and although I finally had some savings I didn't have nearly enough to attend those institutions. With the financial aid I received, Maine fit my budget.

I was the baby of the family and by the time I hit junior high, attending college was the expectation in our home. I say this with great appreciation to my mother and older siblings, because such expectations were not the same for them, or many of their friends. The more likely route for most of them was going straight to work or enlisting in the military. For me, it was evident early on that education represented the most likely express lane off The Hill.

I also needed to go away to college. Get away from 60 Kellogg Street. Get away from the specter of my father. College would be my opportunity to reset, to spread my wings, and to live life without bumping into my old man or into someone who knew about my home life. I was so self-conscious, it was almost paralyzing and it definitely stunted my social growth and affected my confidence.

So, in the fall of 1979, I headed north to Orono. Like many college freshmen, I didn't know what I wanted to do. The only subject I knew much about was sports, but that wasn't offered as a major course of study. My financial aid package included a work-study job and I found one putting ads together for the student newspaper, *The Maine Campus*. It was an interesting job and it gave me a little spending money. It also opened my eyes to the world of journalism. As luck would have it, the sports editor of the newspaper, Dale, and the sports director of the radio station, Tony, lived in my dorm. One morning Dale asked me if I'd be interested in writing track and cross-country articles for the paper. Plenty of students wanted to write about the more popular sports like football, basketball, hockey, and baseball, but not many people wanted to write about the other sports, like track. I quickly became the go-to guy for all lesser-known sports. Tony lived next to me in Chadbourne Hall. We talked about sports all the time, so he knew I was knowledgeable. When he began recruiting students to broadcast reports on WMEB-FM, he asked if I'd be interested. Yes!

I was at the station taping a practice broadcast. I thought it was going well, until Tony dropped to the floor laughing (literally).

I glared at him. "What's so funny?"

He gathered himself and played back the tape. I was so nervous my hands were shaking and you could hear the paper rustling in the background.

"Don't worry about it, you'll be fine," he said.

Then he grabbed the copy and started shaking it, aping my broadcast and cackling. Since we were friends I got the gig, even though I probably didn't deserve it. In the end it was all good; I was starting to come out of my shell and I got to talk about sports.

For my freshman and sophomore years I lived in Chadbourne Hall, one of the older dorms on campus. I landed in a forced triple with two guys from Lewiston who requested to room together, so I assumed I would be the odd man out. Our room was tiny. Open the door and, voila, you could touch it all. Well, not quite, but the room was basically split in half. From front to back was a narrow closet, the bedding (one side had bunks), and a desk and chair. When I got my roommate notice, I assumed I had been placed with two brothers, Mike Lecompte and Norm Lecomte. I figured the missing "p" in Norm's last name was a typo. Both Mike and Norm arrived early and, as expected, left me with the top bunk and a split closet. The windowsill would have to serve as my desk shelf. It all worked out fine since I didn't bring much with me. It would have been great to get there early and nab the single bed, but that was out of my control. We did not own a car, so I scrambled to get myself and my measly belongings to Orono. Fortunately, a Portland High School classmate had wheels and was also in Chadbourne Hall. He was assigned to a double room and he wasn't in any great rush to get there, so Mike and Norm claimed their spots hours before I arrived.

As it turned out the spellings on the notice were correct and Mike and Norm were not related. And, although they asked the university to live together, they were not close friends. However, they were both big partiers in high school—Norm a smoker and Mike a drinker. Both were personable and athletic, and played on the state champion Lewiston High School football team. It was a good triple, and we got along well. Still, as other students dropped out and space opened in the dorm, I expected to move out eventually. In mid-November, just before Thanksgiving break, both guys approached me privately and asked if I'd like to room with them next semester.

Awkward.

I had about a week to decide. To be honest, the choice was clear-cut. During our first month together Mike and I clashed. One afternoon I played tackle football on the quad and I "borrowed" his white cleats. It was raining and muddy, and I returned them grimy. Mike flipped out. I presumed he hated my guts. I should not have taken his cleats without asking and he had every right to be pissed. I kept my distance for weeks.

Norm was a peculiar guy. He frequently got high in high school, and he partied all the time. But in college, he planned to go cold turkey. I respected his decision and commitment, but in doing so, he stopped socializing. He spent most of his time running, often twice a day, or at the library. He was turning over a new leaf and had no patience or interest in what most freshmen, like me, wanted to do. On the other hand, although Mike also wanted to clean up his act, he had no intention of going cold turkey. So most weekends, Norm headed off to the library and we looked for fun around campus. I had more in common with Mike than Norm, so rooming with Mike going forward was the easy choice, but frankly, choosing really sucked.

Chadbourne Hall, specifically the third floor, was great. Nearly everyone wanted to party, but only after taking care of business in the classroom. There was a cast of characters, and I didn't have to stray too far to be entertained. Across the hall were Bruce and Steve, two engineers-in-training who always had a fully stocked refrigerator. They studied hard, partied hard, and willingly shared beers with us lowly freshmen. Their open-door policy was enticing to a kid who'd started late and wanted to be more social. In their room I learned to play drinking games like "quarters" and "bullshit."

At the end of the hall was Klino. If your goal was to get high his room was the place to go. Smoking pot wasn't for me. I had said "No" the one time I was offered a joint in high school. Nevertheless, I dropped in on Klino's room for the cultural education alone. He had all the paraphernalia. His most eye-popping pieces were bongs. One weekend night I sauntered into the room and spotted a four-foot tall bong standing on the floor next to the coffee table. I had never seen anything like it.

"What is that?" I asked.

After giving me crap for being a dumb shit, Klino directed me to take a hit. I did, but don't recall feeling anything (I probably didn't inhale). My competitive juices were aroused so I was compelled to try just for the challenge of it.

We'd all sit in Klino's room and relay race pitchers of beer, and insist that he be the anchor. Klino could open his throat and pour down a beer in seconds. He was the king of the "Hardcore Club," which meant he could drink a thirty-two ounce mug of beer without stopping. I never made it into the club. I failed numerous times.

I lived in Chadbourne Hall for two years at a time when the University of Maine was ranked one of the nation's top party schools. In the early 1980s, there weren't many rules in place to prevent parties. We regularly hauled kegs up to our dorm rooms for parties that attracted students from across campus. When I returned to Orono for my sophomore year, the chatter on campus was that the university planned to clamp down on keg parties and student drinking. On the first weekend back our resident director took his assistants out for dinner and drinks. The campus was eerily quiet since everyone had received the anti-drinking message (at least to start the year.) So what did the clowns on third floor Chadbourne do while the resident staff was away? Get the year started off right. A friend and I drove down to Discount Beverage, bought a keg, and threw a party, inviting everyone within earshot. Before long we needed more kegs. More than a hundred people gathered in our rooms and in the hall, clamoring for drinks. At one point I walked into my room and saw a dozen revelers playing drinking games around our lobster-trap coffee table. I didn't know any of them. The party was out of control, but with no resident assistants around, it was just getting started. A couple of hours later a friend from high school showed up and told me the campus was dead, except here. He'd heard about the party all the way over at Bangor Community College, which was miles away. Thankfully, the residence staff stayed out late and we avoided getting caught or even getting into trouble.

Obviously, when it came to alcohol I was clearly ignoring my father's history, my family's history. and my mother's constant declaration that had instilled fear and helped keep me straight in high school: "If you drink, you will end up just like your father; living on the streets." I was just two hours or so from Munjoy Hill, but it might as well have been a different country—for the first time in my life I felt free from the personal baggage of home and I was gaining confidence. Drinking alcohol helped, I guess.

I drank heavily four nights a week. Every Wednesday there was a party from 11 p.m. to 2 a.m. at the Phi Gamma Delta fraternity house, better known as Fiji; Thursday night was trivia night at the Oronoka restaurant; Friday night we stumbled and bumbled along fraternity row, and we reserved Saturday for all-day drinking. Surprisingly, all this partying didn't affect my classwork much, since Fridays were light days and Sundays were for recovering. It sounds strange, but we were disciplined enough to not party Sunday through Tuesday. And even on Wednesday nights I'd study at the library until ten before traipsing down to Fiji to kick off the "weekend." These were good times.

The summer after my freshman year provided me with a break from all the partying. It was easy to drink on campus, but in the real world the drinking age was 21, and as an 18-year-old without a fake I.D., I couldn't really hit the Portland bars. However, probably the biggest reason I reined in the wild drinking was that I met my first love, Bobbi. In April, Mike and I had hitched from Orono to the University of Maine at Farmington to visit my sister Carolyn and her boyfriend, Paul. I was excited because I wanted to party with my sister. I still hadn't forgiven myself for getting sick and not making it to her friend's party back in high school. After attending a Jonathan Edwards concert, we were at a campus party when I spied Bobbi and a friend sitting on a couch. Mike and I strolled over to meet the girls. Bobbi and I clicked immediately. She was a year younger than me so she was still in high school. She lived in the Portland area and I left with her phone number and I promised to call. Back in Orono, I made the call to set up a date when I returned home.

Setting up the actual date was difficult. I had my driver's license, I didn't have a car. Although Bobbi had wheels, I wanted to provide the transportation for our first date. My sister-in-law Mel saved me again. For my high school senior prom, Mel let me take her red Firebird, which felt awesome. Once I scheduled the date with Bobbi, Mel was my first call. She couldn't say yes fast enough. Her quick reaction was understandable since Mel always gave me a hard time about my lack of social activity in high school. I spent most Friday and Saturday nights at home. I was anti-drinking and embarrassed by my surroundings, so I chose to stay in rather than risk being called out. Mel would give me grief, in a nice way, for staying at home studying on weekend nights. I'm sure she thought I was odd.

One of our best moments that summer was my sister Carolyn's wedding. I brought Bobbi and was very proud to show her off. The wedding reception was at St. Paul's Episcopal Church on Congress Street across from the Levinsky's store, and next to the Cathedral. It was very intimate, just family and close friends. My father was not invited to the wedding. I wasn't consulted, but I fully supported his omission.

Bobbi and I had a great summer together, at some point even expressing our love for each other. I think I can also speak for her when I say we didn't know what we were doing. I know I didn't. She was my first serious girlfriend, but it didn't last long because I was selfish. We started drifting apart when I went back to college. She was enjoying her senior year in high school, while I was having fun as a sophomore at Orono. We talked often, but rarely saw each other. I did have the built-in excuse of not having a car, so I couldn't just drive home, but it was more than that. I just didn't want to go home every weekend or even every other weekend. That disinterest led to some bad phone calls, and by Thanksgiving we knew it was over. We exchanged Christmas presents, broke up, and never talked again. I screwed this up. She was a great gal, and I was immature.

In addition to dating my first serious girlfriend, two other major events occurred in the summer of 1980.

Walt's good friend, David, was stabbed only a few feet from our front door. It was around midnight, and Bobbi was bringing me home after a date. As we drove up Congress Street I saw an ambulance with flashing lights at the corner of Kellogg and Congress streets. We detoured to my house and Bobbi headed back home.

I found my mother on the steps crying. David was stabbed multiple times, and it was still touch and go whether he would survive. David, like my brother Walt, opted to stay on The Hill after graduation rather than go to college or join the military. He quickly became a fixture on The Corner, and before long he was involved in a few shady operations. The neighborhood assumed the stabbing was a drug deal or bad bet gone wrong. But it was a case of being in the wrong place at the wrong time. David and Teddy were leaving The Corner for a nightcap at George's Tavern. As they passed an apartment building they stumbled upon a domestic dispute playing out on the street. As a screaming woman ran to call the police, her pissed boyfriend came up behind David and stuck a knife just under his left clavicle, only inches from his heart. David lived, although it would take years before he really recovered. David succumbed to multiple addictions. It happened so fast, we were all in denial. It was another example of the struggles people faced on Munjoy Hill.

The second event was even more shocking.

My father was engaged.

After his final rehab at Togus, Walter stayed at his sister's place in Portland for a short time and then moved in with Ann, the intern who worked as his psychologist at Togus. Ann, also divorced with children of her own, had a first husband who was abusive, so she had cut him loose. Walter, sober for the first time in years, began talking to Ann about marriage soon after leaving the hospital. She had left an abusive husband and here she was opening her door to a seventeen-year street rat, a man who had failed miserably at being a husband and father.

Walter started working as a handyman, painting houses and laying bricks with old friends, which kept him busy during the day while Ann was at work. Friends picked him up in the morning and

This is me in my fraternity room at the University of Maine.

brought him home at night. He didn't take any detours, and Ann was always waiting for him.

A problem for Walter was that he and my mother were not actually divorced. When Ma sent him packing in 1963, there was no talk of divorce. Ma hoped he would straighten up, not necessarily so he could come back to our house, but just so he could get off the streets and live a normal life. She didn't care about getting divorced—after two failed marriages and eight kids, finding another man was the last thing on her wish list. She quickly granted his request.

I guess the news about my father was a good thing, but I had no faith in him. I assumed this latest attempt at sobriety would meet the same fate as the rest—complete and utter failure. I also felt the whole marriage thing was a slap in the face to my mother. For seventeen years, he wouldn't or couldn't straighten up his act for her or for us kids, but suddenly he could beat it just like that? Now that we were all grown and he didn't have any responsibilities, he could stop drinking on a dime? I realize I sound bitter, but I really wasn't. I was defensive of my mother. I had moved on from my father. Any feelings I had for the man were suppressed.

Regardless, less than a year after he was released from Togus in wake of his fifth brush with death because of alcohol abuse, my father and Ann were married. It was a small ceremony. None of his children were invited.

I didn't even know it was happening.

Chapter Eleven
Out of the Shadows

A s I neared the end of sophomore year in the spring of 1981, I faced two pressing decisions—declaring a major and finding a new place to live in Orono. Since I enjoyed working at *The Maine Campus* and doing football, basketball, and baseball commentary for WMEB, I decided to double major in journalism and broadcasting. Once I had begun to speak up, it was clear that I had a strong voice and was comfortable talking about sports. I figured with proper training I could become a professional sportscaster.

Choosing where to live was complicated. Mike, my roommate, was finishing his two-year forestry program, and was not returning to Orono. I could stay in a dorm for another year, rent an off-campus apartment, or join a fraternity. Returning to the dorm didn't appeal to me. It was the most expensive option and none of my friends would be there, so I ruled that out.

I agreed to sign for an apartment in York Village with five friends. York Village was an apartment complex owned by and adjacent to the university, but was considered off-campus housing. Although I wasn't sold on York Village, the guys needed my John Hancock since six signatures were required on the rental contract. I agreed to add my name, but made it clear I was considering other options.

I also continued to consider joining a fraternity. I had received bids to join Phi Gamma Delta (Fiji), and Alpha Tau Omega (ATO) in early spring. I had friends in Fiji. I was excited about both houses, but couldn't afford them. Both Fiji and ATO, located side by side on College Avenue, had "very Greek," reputations, meaning they were heavily invested in Greek Life and actively participated in local and national fraternal events. That was cool, but it came with a high cost. I couldn't swing the room and board, never mind any extra Greek fees. Money wasn't the only reason I passed on Fiji and ATO. While both houses were popular and hosted frequent parties, they were both preppy and that posed a problem. I didn't own any "alligator shirts" or pants, and I wasn't in a position to upgrade my wardrobe. I couldn't picture myself sporting a preppy logo like Lacoste. I was still too insecure and short on confidence. Yes, I was getting better, but at times I still thought, "Who am I kidding? I'm just white trash from Munjoy Hill." Two popular fraternities welcomed me, but I couldn't get out of my own way.

I was still undecided where I would live my junior year, when my friend Randy came to my door on a Friday night in April. I opened the door to find my old friend and three of his Sigma Nu brothers. Sigma Nu was better known as The Zoo.

"Hey, we're having a party at the house," Randy barked. "Let's go!"

"Now?"

"Yeah, we gotta move."

I grabbed a coat and didn't ask any more questions.

The Sigma Nu house sat on the other side of campus and was rather nondescript. The house had approximately twenty brothers, while most fraternities had forty to sixty, and it was light on amenities. There wasn't any furniture in the house and the structure, both inside and out, was in desperate need of repair. Randy had joined the frat the previous year and claimed the house was rebounding.

This "party" was no ordinary get together. There were about thirty guys there and plenty of beer, but no girls. Turns out it was a Sigma Nu rush event. Basically, unbeknownst to me, I was auditioning for a bid. The three guys with Randy were on the recruitment committee, and were hunting for possible brothers to join. I had been to a few Friday night parties at The Zoo, so I was familiar with the place. There was nothing preppy about this group. The common attire was sweats, and they were as anti-Greek as possible and still be a Greek house. The house was known and popular because it hosted great parties where all were welcome.

After the rush event, I was extended a bid to join. I said "yes." It was an easy decision. Considering the limited amenities offered, the cost of living at the house was a bargain. Randy already lived in the house and was looking for a roommate, so everything fell into place. I was psyched that the housing search was over. All was well.

Summer back in Portland was relatively routine. I worked at the Surplus Store in Monument Square. When it came to summer jobs during college, this was unquestionably my favorite. It was an active place with customers, including many friends and family, dropping in to mingle and peruse the goods. The work itself was busy; basically making a sale, keeping the shelves tidy, and regularly running up and down the stairs to restock inventory. I always looked forward to inventory runs since Dickie Ward, a local basketball legend, managed the storeroom and would always stop whatever he was doing to talk smack about sports. Meanwhile, more knowledgeable co-workers like Ken and Brian, who could never slip away, managed the heavy lifting in fishing and camping.

In previous years my walk to and from Monument Square was disheartening. However, this summer was serene. With my father now married, I didn't fear seeing him in all his drunken glory on India Street or in Lincoln Park. No matter how much I tried not to care, it had still made me sad to see him and he was always on my mind when I was in that area. Although I admit I did expect him to fall off the wagon and be back on the streets soon.

While my radar was always up when it came to my father, any self-awareness about the problems of alcohol seemed to escape me when I looked in the mirror. After work I regularly went out with my Surplus Store buddies, primarily Brian and Tim, to pound beers. We had thrown in some crazy nights on the town. The most ridiculous thing we did that summer was play eighteen holes of golf in the Old Port. Of course, there is no golf course in the Old Port, but it provided the ideal "course" for a drinking game. My friend Skate outlined the rules, although they were pretty simple—in a single night, each player had to drink one full beer at eighteen different bars. We teed off at Forest Gardens and then drank at a few places near the University of Southern Maine campus, before taxiing into the Old Port to finish our round. We hit Bill's Pizza "at the turn" and I vaguely remember J's Oyster Bar and Kayo's serving as the seventeenth and eighteenth holes. We completed the round, but that's about all I recall. I spent most of the summer staggering around the Old Port; it was not a good look and the irony was completely lost on me.

Back at Orono that fall, I picked up where I left off. We tapped kegs at the frat house daily. As a new pledge, my job was to make sure we never ran out of beer. While some fraternities required long, drawn-out pledge periods, being a pledge at Sigma Nu was stress-free. Other frats required pledges to do often silly things like dressing up for class or waiting hand and foot on the brothers, and I am sure there must have been some harsher hazing as well. But at Sigma Nu, I don't recall any hazing and the only thing we did that even resembled it was during Hell Week, the traditional final week of pledging. On that Monday, we, the six pledges, got hauled out of bed at six in the morning for a three-mile run. We were supposed to do that all week, but by Wednesday, none of the actual brothers were getting up to run, so three of us pledges blew it off and went back to bed. The three pledges who did run were pissed, but the brothers told them that we (the non-runners) were the smart ones. That was the extent of our Hell Week and initiation night was just one big party. I've heard horror stories about hazing and am grateful that Sigma Nu didn't bother.

The brothers didn't haze, but they could party. The fraternity was wild. During my junior year we bought twenty-plus kegs and entertained more than seven hundred revelers every other Friday night. The Zoo was so popular that university students added it to their calendars and harassed us for tickets weeks in advance. It was the place to be on Friday night, in part because everyone was welcome. We didn't discriminate. Whoever scored a ticket was in. Our social chairman would dish out ten to fifteen tickets per brother, then distribute the rest to women on campus. Security was important, because fights would regularly break out at other fraternity parties, and that turned people, especially college girls, away. We didn't have that problem at The Zoo. The reason: Peter, the strongest man on campus and an offensive lineman on the football team, was a Sigma Nu.

The football fraternity, or at least the fraternity with the most football players, was Tau Kappa Epsilon (TEKE). Those boys had the well-earned reputation of causing trouble at parties around campus. They were banned from having parties themselves, so they were always out cruising. They were present at our Friday night bashes. Peter and his fellow linemen from TEKE would work the door, so we never had any issues. This worked out great for me. Since I was one of the smaller guys in the house, I never had door duty. I worked the bar, which was a blast. The lines at the bar were steadily three to four deep and it was easy being the hero, getting refills for friends or the pretty girl a few rows back.

Everything outside the fraternity house was going well, too. I was pleased with my decision to double major in journalism and broadcasting, and I continued to gain experience writing columns and being on air. Most of my written pieces were still about the school's athletes who played secondary sports. One afternoon our editor called me into his office to review a story I'd written on the school's 800-meter state record holder. I was nervous because in the feature I had gotten cute quoting the track coach, and thought maybe it was ill advised. Fortunately that wasn't it at all. He wanted to congratulate me, since the story was picked up by a regional running magazine and would run in its next issue. My byline in a professional publication. That was cool.

When not in class or writing a column, I was at the campus radio station. I had become sports director at WMEB, meaning I set the programming and assigned the staff. I took full advantage of my position and named myself the student voice of Maine football, basketball, and baseball. While hockey was a huge sport at Maine, I didn't broadcast hockey games because I didn't know anything about the sport. That was confirmed the one time I sat in as a color analyst and kept calling the puck a ball, and the periods, quarters. It was embarrassing. I barely uttered two words after the first period.

And we continued to drink heavily. My roommate Randy was often out of control. He always pushed the envelope, and I was usually a dependable sidekick. Randy was a six-foot, three-inch, blond-haired, blue-eyed wise-ass, a junk thrower from Rhode Island who came to Maine hoping to play baseball. The Maine baseball teams in the early 1980s regularly advanced to the College World Series and the teams were stacked. Frankly, there was too much talent for a walk-on to succeed, so Randy gave up his baseball dream after his freshman year. Today, he is a successful businessman, husband, and father of three. But I think he was lucky to make it out of college alive.

Randy was the most sarcastic person I ever met and just as witty. His constant sarcasm grated on some of our friends, but I found it funny and enjoyed his company tremendously. If we weren't studying at the library, we were playing intramurals or looking for a party. In the early '80s nobody had really heard of Mothers Against Drunk Driving (MADD) or Students Against Drunk Driving (SADD), or at least we hadn't. Drinking and driving was commonplace. Although times were changing, getting behind the wheel shit-faced wasn't considerd that big of a deal. It was still the "one for the road era" and everybody did it. I still didn't own a car, but Randy drove a Chevy Blazer.

One winter night we partied in Bangor. While driving home Randy decided to play chicken. To him this meant racing up a hill on the wrong side of the road until he reached the crest. I'm serious. There were many sizable hills in Bangor. By this time, it was around two in the morning, so there weren't many cars out on the roads. He found a hill, raced up on the wrong side of the road and flew over the apex. I freaked out in the passenger seat, and screamed at him, "Cut the shit."

He ignored me, laughed it off, and found another hill. Just before we hit the crown I saw headlights. Randy swerved to narrowly dodge the oncoming car, cackling while trying to regain control. I was hysterical. He wouldn't listen to me, he was looking for another hill. I didn't know what to do, so I started crying. I'm guessing this startled him, because he realized his madness and drove home.

Later in the year, after a small party at the house, he grabbed me and said, "Let's go to Mickey D's." McDonald's was about two miles away in Old Town and stayed open late doing big business with drunken students. We were regular patrons. Is it any wonder that I gained forty pounds in college? Between a meal plan that offered twenty-one meals a week and midnight runs to McDonald's, plus all the beer, I'm lucky I only gained forty. I can't remember why I passed on this midnight run, but it was the right call. Randy hopped in his Blazer without me and arrived at the restaurant in one piece. During his return, less than a half-mile from Sigma Nu, he caught an edge in the road and flipped the Blazer. It rolled over multiple times before landing within yards of the Stillwater River. Miraculously, he suffered only minor injuries, but the Blazer was totaled. That was Randy's wake-up call. We definitely slowed down following his accident. He didn't have a car anymore, so that kept us on campus for the most part. Randy, who was on schedule to graduate that year, cut back on the drinking and started focusing on his future.

During all this, Walter was secretly stalking me. In the fall of 1981, Ann enrolled in a master's program at the University of Maine. They were renting an apartment in Orono. My father was working as a custodian at Husson College in Bangor. I had no idea.

He would sit in his car across from the fraternity house and watch me walk back and forth to class. Walter wanted to approach me, but didn't know how to do it. He was scared.

The last time I actually stood face to face with him was that horrible morning at the bus stop in Lincoln Park during my freshman year of high school. He was begging my friends for money—so wasted that he didn't even recognize me. I turned and ran through Portland as fast as I could to get away from him. I had not spoken to him since that day. I got nervous just walking through the park, fearing I would see the man. I had avoided him at all costs. It was evident that I wanted nothing to do with him. Part of the reason I was coming out of my shell at Orono was because I thought he was nowhere around and I wouldn't ever see him. Walter had other ideas.

After stalking me for a while, Walter made his move on a Sunday afternoon in April 1982. I was sitting in my room with Randy when we heard a knock on the door. It was my fraternity "big brother" Brent announcing, "Your father is downstairs in the dining room."

I assumed he was talking to Randy, so I continued to do my thing as Randy climbed out of bed to go downstairs.

Brent said to Randy, "Not your father, Ed's father."

"Mine?"

"That's what he said. He's at the dining table."

"Tell him I'll be right down."

I was stunned.

The room fell silent.

Finally, Randy asked, "Should I offer him a beer?"

It was the perfect response. Randy was probably the only person on campus who knew anything about my father and our history. He realized immediately that I didn't see this coming and it made me laugh.

The walk from my room to the dining area was approximately one hundred feet, but it took me about ten minutes. First, I went into the bathroom. I just needed a minute. Staring blankly in the mirror, I doused my face with water. I was perplexed. Thoughts raced through my mind.

"Is he shit-faced?"

"Is he in some kind of trouble?"

"Did this Ann lady smarten up and send him packing?"

"What the hell does he want?"

None of this made any sense.

I had been haunted and embarrassed by this man for two decades. I thought I was finally free of him, and now he was sitting downstairs in my frat house.

From the top of the fraternity's winding staircase I could see most of the dining room, but not my father. Once I reached the bottom of the stairwell I caught a glimpse of the back of a gray-haired man sitting at the end of the table. From behind, he looked good, but I didn't want to get my hopes up. Even though it was early in the day, he'd probably been drinking, I thought. Just as I crossed into the room my father turned around and stood up.

He looked fabulous. His healthy, sober appearance knocked the wind out of me. I was speechless. I nodded. He extended his hand which was shaking visibly. He asked if we could talk.

I eyed him skeptically. I shook his hand and said, "Sure."

His shaking puzzled me. Was it nerves or another detox phase? I sat down.

"This is a surprise."

Walter smiled.

"I'm sure you weren't expecting me. Is this a good time?"

"Yeah, just studying up in my room."

I embarrassingly pointed to the new sofa and chairs stacked in the far corner of the living room. We had the room to ourselves.

"We had a party last night, and the furniture hasn't been moved back."

I got to the point.

"What are you doing here?"

"Well, that's a long story," he said. "But first, thanks for seeing me. Your mother told me that the last time you saw me was in Lincoln Park. I don't remember it, but I'm sure it was bad."

"It was awful. You had no idea it was me."

"I'm sorry, very sorry. I would have understood if you didn't come down."

He got more emotional.

"I've been sober for over two years. The longest stretch of my life. It's been tough, but I know I can't go back there again. I got married almost a year ago. Your mom was great, no questions asked. She deserved better."

"Yes, she did."

He acknowledged my response.

"I met Ann, my wife, while drying out at Togus. She was working there; we hit it off and started dating. We tied the knot last summer. Ann is getting her master's in psychology here at Maine. We live in an apartment in Orono, and I work as a janitor at Husson College in Bangor. I'm feeling pretty good."

"You look good, you really do," I said. "Ann sounds amazing."

"Thanks. I've been trying to work up the nerve to come talk to you. I have spied on you around campus a few times. Thought about just saying 'Hi,' but I figured that would be awkward."

Nervous laughter.

"This is much better. …. So, you've been stalking me?"

Getting my humor, he said, "Only from afar. I was nervous. Part of me expected you to push away, and I didn't want to deal with that. Not sure I'm ready now, but felt the time was right to risk it. Again, thanks for seeing me."

Of his three children, I was the most distant and unforgiving. I was being protective of myself and Ma; he thought I was insensitive. It was probably a little of both. But there was no question that I had no respect for the man, and he knew it.

My father described his last few years in great detail.

After relocating to Orono in the summer of 1981, my father had trouble finding any work. After months of rejection, he landed a custodial job at Husson College. They loved him. He often took on duties that were neglected by others, but needed to be done. Not surprisingly, he became their go-to guy very quickly. He knew being a janitor wasn't a glamorous gig. At Cathedral, I remember kids making fun of the janitor, dismissing the role and the person doing it as nobody. Walter understood this, but what was a 50-year-old guy with an eighth-grade education, no work history, and a twenty-year stint as a drunk going to do? He knew he was fortunate to get this job, and he embraced it.

I think he realized that it wasn't all about him. This was Ann's time, about getting her degree and building a future. For perhaps the first time in his life he put somebody else first.

I listened and took it all in. I didn't really know what to say. I was intrigued and I guess happy for him, but guarded.

Finally, my father got to the big reason for his visit.

"So, why am I here? Well, now that I'm in recovery I was hoping to have a relationship with my son."

Another moment or two of uncomfortable silence.

"Not sure I'm ready for that. To be candid, I don't know what I want. I certainly didn't expect, after all this time, for you to walk in here today. Frankly, I prepared myself to never see you again. Figured I'd get a phone call from Ma or somebody telling me you were dead. When that happened, I'd think about it a minute, do whatever was expected, and move on. I didn't think it would be very emotional, just closure.

"This is different. You really do look great. I was dreading coming down the stairs. Figured you'd be drunk, embarrassing me again. I really did think that. Sorry. I hoped it would be different. This is nice. I'm happy for you. I'm proud of you. But, I have a long memory and very little of it is good."

More awkward silence.

I broke it.

"What are you expecting?"

"You've already given it to me. We've had a chance to talk. I probably didn't even deserve that. Like I said, I would love to have a relationship with you. I don't know what that looks like, or even means, but that's what I want. I'm hoping, maybe you can come over for dinner, meet Ann, catch up a little more. Make up for some lost time."

"Let me think about it." I hesitated, before adding, "I don't think you can make up for lost time. It's gone, never to return. I can't imagine how hard it was for you to walk through that door today. You had every reason to fear the worst. We don't have a relationship, never have. Not sure I even want one. I don't think I'm ready to just forgive and forget. I really need time to process this. I'm sorry, but I hope you understand."

"I do."

Walter wrote down his phone number and address and handed them to me.

"When you're ready, please call. Again, thanks for seeing me today. I apologize for the surprise."

My father leaned in and gave me a hug before walking out the door.

It was a nice visit, but I was confused. My father wanted me to dine with him and his wife and act like a happy family? I had a hard time with that. My biggest concern was my mother. Although she never never appeared to hold any grudges toward him, I assumed she must be bitter and angry with this situation. She didn't waver granting his divorce wish, but how would she feel about me welcoming him back with open arms? She said she didn't care an iota, but I didn't believe her. I used her as an excuse to keep my father at bay.

In May, I reluctantly went to my father's apartment for dinner. I timed it just before heading home for the summer so that I would soon be gone. I had reservations about his marriage, and was unsure about my feelings toward Ann. I thought it was only a matter of time before my father screwed up again and I wasn't interested in a stepmother.

Dinner was delicious and Ann was gracious. She was proper and confident, the antithesis of Walter. Ann was a psychologist-in-training, but fortunately toned it down for the evening. The get-together was about Walter connecting with his son, and she was an amiable wallflower. Ann was not what I expected physically, not that I had any visions beforehand. She was plain, yet imposing. At first glance, she appeared to tower over Walter, when in reality they were about the same size. While Walter slumped, she carried herself, especially her broad shoulders, regally. Ann was an attractive woman, but there was an intimidating aura about her that reminded me of Nurse Ratched from the movie *One Flew Over the Cuckoo's Nest*.

I sat there thinking, "How did these two get together?"

After dinner we exchanged pleasantries, and I promised to reconnect in the fall when I returned to school. I successfully danced around any deep conversation.

Chapter Twelve
Wake-Up Call

The year 1982 was a confusing time for me. In April, my father, much to my surprise, walked back into my life and I was trying to understand the meaning of it all. He had let me down so many times I didn't want to be set up for more disappointment. He went from out of sight, out of mind, to constantly in my thoughts.

In May, during finals week I went to Pat's Pizza with a few friends. Two tables away sat a group of college girls enjoying pizza and beers. I recognized only one of the girls, but sitting beside her was, in my humble opinion, one of the most beautiful girls on campus.

By this time in my life, I had gained even more confidence, so approaching and flirting with girls (most of them, anyway) was comfortable and fun. I moseyed over, said hello to the girl I knew, and began chatting with the group. They invited us to join them. Jeanne, the focus of my attention, was a stunning blonde. I learned she was from the Portland suburb of Falmouth and would be living at home for the summer. No longer one to waste time or the opportunity, I politely asked for her telephone number.

Once back at home, we connected and went out on a few dates. I thought we clicked and had a nice thing going. Falmouth is an affluent town that borders Portland. Route 88 runs through

Falmouth Foreside, which is the part of Falmouth along the Atlantic Ocean lined with majestic homes. Jeanne's home was on the water in Falmouth Foreside. It was grand. From her front yard, I could see Munjoy Hill across the bay. Her parents, both doctors, were welcoming, although they were inquisitive and protective of their little girl. Jeanne was unpretentious, and I previously had no idea of her family's wealth. I didn't share a lot with them, but my responses to her parents' well-intentioned inquiries made it clear my station was a bit different.

The distance between Falmouth Foreside and the heart of Munjoy Hill in 1982 was not just the other side of the tracks, they were different worlds. A little while after I visited Falmouth Foreside, we were on a date and I had to stop by my house on Kellogg Street. I had only planned to jump out of the car for a minute, but Ma was outside and she insisted we visit. We stayed there for about an hour, so Jeanne spent some quality time with my mom and her sixteen house pets. After our date, I took her back to Falmouth. I never saw her again. It is possible that she just grew tired of me, so I can't say for sure why it fizzled, but bringing anybody, let alone a girl, back to 60 Kellogg Street was risky.

Having completed my junior year of college, I started to concentrate a little more on the future. I was on track to graduate in the spring, but I needed an internship to fulfill requirements. I landed a summer internship with WGAN (which later became WGME) in Portland. The television station was located in North Deering, about four miles from home, inconvenient since I still didn't have a car. I worked two nights a week from the six o'clock broadcast until the eleven o'clock news. I also worked five to six days a week at the Surplus Store. I used my thumb to get back and forth. The time window to get from one job to the next was tight, so taking the bus wouldn't work. At least I was familiar with the route. I would start on Washington Avenue, just like going to Cheverus, and end at the Northport Plaza. During the day, traffic was busy and I always got a quick lift, so getting to Channel 13 wasn't a problem. The bigger issue was getting home at night. Hitching a ride at that hour was hit or miss, mostly miss. There weren't many cars and even fewer people were willing to pick me up. Most nights I had to walk the four miles home.

One night a middle-aged man, slight in stature, pulled up just as I was leaving the station and offered me a lift. We got a few blocks down the road when he asked, "Where does one go to meet other guys around here?"

I wasn't prepared for this and stuttered a bit, suggesting "Deering Oaks, maybe?"

Deering Oaks is a picturesque park in the center of the city that had a reputation as a spot for gay men to meet. I really wasn't sure, but it sounded like good advice at the time. He seemed to appreciate the tip, but then got personal.

"Have you ever tried it (pointing down to his crotch, suggesting a blow job)?"

I looked at him.

"No!"

He smiled.

"If you try it, you might like it."

At this point my insides were churning. I tried to stay calm. Since I was bigger than this guy I wasn't afraid, but I was unnerved.

"I don't think so."

As we approached Tukey's Bridge I strongly suggested, "Pull over on the other side of the bridge and let me out. If you continue down to Forest Avenue, Deering Oaks is right there."

He pulled over and let me out at the fork in the road before Munjoy Hill. That was the last time I hitchhiked at night. The rest of the summer I used my legs and ran home from WGAN.

I turned 21 in late July. The evening began early, around four, when my friend Coop arrived. He brought a fifth of vodka and we began doing shots. We were in town by seven and we were hitting our favorite spots (Kayo's, Eric's, and the Old Port Tavern). My night didn't last long. I was home in bed by one in the morning. At some point we split up and lost track of each other. I only remember two things. The first was waking up next to a green dumpster in some alley, and the second was rounding the corner of Kellogg and Congress streets staggering home. The night was nearly a total blackout. I figured out a few days later that the dumpster was behind Kayo's bar. My best guesstimate is that I was feeling sick and went searching for a secluded spot to throw up. I assume I stumbled out of Kayo's up the adjacent alley and passed out next to the dumpster. I have no idea how long I was there, but do remember laying on the ground beside the green monster. Once again, the irony of my issues with my dad and sleeping next to the dumpster were lost on me at the time.

The next thing I recall was turning the corner for home. It is a good mile from Kayo's to Kellogg Street, and I surely staggered the whole way. I was shocked nobody recognized me or said anything, but evidently I went unnoticed.

The only reason I knew I was home by one was Coop. Ma was fairly oblivious. My only guess is she was asleep when I got home, since she claimed not to hear me come in. I made a beeline to the bathroom to puke, and grabbed a bucket to put next to my bed. Since this wasn't my first rodeo, I had the drill down. Apparently,

Coop was worried and came by the house looking for me. He got there at about one o'clock. He didn't know what to do.

He wondered, "Do I knock on the door and see if he is home?" He opted not to do that, concerned if I wasn't there, he'd upset my mother. Instead he spent the night in his car outside our house waiting for me. I found him sleeping there the next morning. We had a good laugh, and fortunately nobody was hurt.

Days before my birthday I had to renew my driver's license. Going to the motor vehicle bureau and waiting in line for hours was a hassle. This visit wasn't any different. Finally my number was called; I paid the fee and lined up for the photo. It was depressing. I barely recognized the guy in the picture. Who was this guy with three chins? I was despondent. Clearly exercise hadn't been on the agenda for a while, since the 170 pounds I listed on the license was a joke. After pocketing the photo I searched for a scale. I was horrified to see it tipping at nearly two hundred pounds.

I had one month to get in shape before classes began. I did double workouts, a run in the morning and another in the evening, every day. I also cut back considerably on alcohol. By the time I moved back into Sigma Nu I was back down to around 180 pounds. I looked better, but I'd have to live with the license photo for years. I thought about the events of my 21st birthday every time I pulled out my license. It was time to shape up in more ways than one.

The first six or seven weeks of senior year were a repeat of junior year. The fraternity picked up right where it left off; we had blow-out parties every other Friday night in September and October. And I was up to the same old tricks. I'd get a good buzz on and flirt the night away. If I was lucky it might lead to more than talk. One October evening it did, and once back in my room I had an epiphany. I remember saying to myself, "What the fuck are you doing?" My behavior was getting old, and it wasn't that fun anymore. I thought back to my birthday, of the spewing mess I'd become, and saw the same thing happening here. It was time to stop partying and get serious about the future. Graduation would come in May, and I had no job prospects. I had even convinced myself that the distraction of a girlfriend could hold me back. That was truly my mindset. Playing around with no commitment was innocuous, but now even that was unfulfilling.

However, there was one girl I'd been admiring for months, but I believed she was out of my league. She was like kryptonite to my newfound confidence. We would talk often, both at parties and the library (really), and she was perfect. Of course, with her I had no confidence, but then I caught a break.

As my fraternity brothers were adjourning a chapter meeting, our treasurer, Jeff, pulled me aside.

"You got a minute, I need to talk to you."

"Yeah, what's up?"

He looked me straight in the eyes and from left field stated, "Do you know who likes you?"

"Maybe ... I don't know, who?"

He shouts, "Marty."

After I coolly brushed it off he added, "Are you fucking nuts!"

Martha Rand! I didn't know what to do with the news that Martha Rand was interested in me. So, I didn't do anything.

Martha "Marty" Rand was a year behind me in school, first at Portland High, then at Maine. I noticed her during my senior year in high school. She had it all. She was beautiful, she was personable, and she was popular. I, on the other hand, felt invisible. At Lyman Moore Middle School she was named "Most Outstanding Girl." She was a talented athlete, a tennis ace, and a natural in soccer, basketball, and softball. At Portland High, she played tennis but gave up the other sports to become a cheerleader, eventually head cheerleader. Portland had the usual cliques in high school: jocks, brains, geeks, stoners, mean girls, etc. Many guys considered cheerleaders the high school "It" girls. Other than an "excuse me" in the doorway to class, I never spoke to Martha, or any other cheerleader for that matter, during my two years at Portland High. I was insecure and simply felt the girls were out of my league.

A year later as a freshman at Orono, I saw Martha again; for a split second. Unknown to me, her older sister Cindy lived on the third floor of Chadbourne Hall. The dorm was split by floor right down the middle, girls on the left and boys on the right. Cindy's room was down the hall, far away from the boys. Cindy was a sophomore and had a boyfriend who lived elsewhere, so I rarely saw her. In fact, I didn't even know her name. Well, it was a Saturday and I was coming back from lunch at the dining commons. Skipping up the stairwell I noticed two girls descending. The girl in front was Cindy, so I probably smiled and quickly looked away. But I looked up again in time to see the other girl; it was Martha looking right at me. She recognized me, smiled, and said, "Hi."

My day was made. She knew who I was. I wasn't invisible after all.

As luck would have it, Martha followed her sister and two older brothers to the University of Maine. I had no idea that she was at Maine her freshman year. I was still in Chadbourne Hall, and she lived across campus in Corbett Hall. Our paths never crossed. My move to Sigma Nu as a junior changed that. Martha's best friend, Peggy, was dating one of my Sigma Nu brothers, so Marty and Peggy were regulars at the fraternity house.

At one of our Friday night parties we finally connected. As Martha and I talked, I was oblivious to all around me. Before I realized it we were the only two people left in the room. It was nearly three in the morning and even the lost souls were gone. We had been talking for hours.

She knew a lot more about me than I suspected. However, the one thing I always tried to hide, where I came from, had remained a secret. When I told her that I lived on Munjoy Hill, she thought I was kidding. She associated me with my high school friends, most of whom lived on the West End. Martha had many friends from The Hill, so she was not put off by my revelation, but it did surprise her. Hill kids had a reputation, often not that good, and sometimes carried themselves with an edgy swagger.

That night changed my life, but, of course, I did nothing. I don't remember everything we talked about, but it was clear we had misconceptions about each other. My stereotype of her was as the head cheerleader, and probably a mean girl. I couldn't have been more wrong. She was beautiful and kind.

Yet my thoughts still were, "Damn, what would she see in me?" and "She's way out of my league."

As I have said, leaving Kellogg Street for college provided a fresh start. It allowed me to escape many of my personal hang-ups and develop relationships on neutral ground, away from the shadows of Walter Crockett and 60 Kellogg Street. I do regret not letting people in during high school. I was too preoccupied with my surroundings and I reckoned keeping them hidden from friends and peers was best.

It was amazing to have my eyes opened, but when it came to Martha, I still lacked the confidence to make a move. Maybe because we both went to Portland High School, some of my confidence issues from high school resurfaced. We often saw each other at parties and at the library and we would catch up and laugh. Talking to Martha was effortless. She was interesting and humorous and a great listener. We'd be at the library and I'd look up at the clock and wonder, "Where did all the time go?"

She was great and we became friends. I stress "friends," because I still didn't believe I had a shot at dating her. Funny thing about the library, I was there often because studying at the fraternity wasn't easy. Martha began going to the library regularly once she discovered I was there. I always sat in the same spot, soft chairs on the second floor, so I was easy to find.

Once we started dating, she admitted that she was constantly at the library not to study, but to see me. My failure to make a move bewildered her. She assumed I wasn't interested. I was clueless, even though the signs were there—playing tennis matches, closing down parties, quizzing me on African capitals. I just thought these were coincidences.

Anyway, Jeff's assertion in the fall of my senior year that Marty was interested in me snapped me out of the doldrums.

"Should I ask her out?"

The obvious answer was yes, but I had a way of overthinking things and making them more complicated. I spent the next few weeks procrastinating and thinking about the future. I'd be graduating in a few months and I didn't want to start anything I thought had long-term potential. My focus needed to be on the job search, not my love life.

Chapter Thirteen
Martha

While mixing tapes at the campus radio station in mid-October, one of my broadcasting professors waved me into his studio.

"Ed, Channel 5 in Bangor called and asked me to send a few students over to audition for the weekend newscast. I think you should consider it."

Of course!

"What do I have to do?"

He directed me to Gordon Manuel, station manager at WABI-TV Channel 5, the local CBS affiliate. I auditioned a week later. The professor recommended three students. One was Jim Morris. Jim was an outstanding broadcaster with a deep voice and a face for television. I figured the job was his to lose. It was. He nailed the audition and was the station's first choice. Fortuitously for me, Jim was already lining up a full-time gig with WVII Channel 7, the ABC affiliate in Bangor, and declined.

Gordon Manuel turned his focus to me. He called on a Tuesday morning.

"Ed, are you available to do the evening broadcast this Saturday?"

I accepted immediately. I couldn't believe my good fortune.

Mom and I under the mistletoe at 60 Kellogg Street.

I called my father and he promised to watch. I would have phoned my mom and siblings first, but they lived beyond the station's signal, so I didn't bother to call them that morning. I hadn't seen much of my father and Ann since I had returned to Orono for my senior year. For some reason, I was feeling a bit guilty about it. I felt I needed to work at keeping the communication lines open, which would be a recurring problem, and I reckoned anchoring the news might camouflage my lame efforts. After all, he could actually see me every weekend, even if it was on television and not in person. I don't think my father missed a broadcast.

My debut broadcast as the weekend anchor of the eleven o'clock news was scheduled for November 6, 1982.

In addition to being nervous about performing live on the air, I was worried about what to wear and how to get to Bangor. Since

I would sit behind a desk as anchor, the audience would only see me from the waist up. Thus, I only had to stress about finding half of a wardrobe. I had some oxford shirts, but no ties, suits, or sports coats. Thankfully, a fraternity brother, Nick, was about my size and supplied me with an array of ties and coats to choose from. He made me look sharp. The next problem was getting to work. WABI was located in Bangor, quite a few miles from campus, and I still didn't have a car. Again, my fraternity brothers bailed me out. I borrowed wheels every Saturday and Sunday night for the first three weeks. Of course, the gas to get to Bangor probably cost more than the five dollars per hour I was paid.

When I went home to Portland for Thanksgiving break, I asked my brother-in-law, Bruce, to take me car shopping. Since I only had about eight hundred dollars in my bank account, my options were limited. At the first car lot, we found a two-toned Ford Granada. It wasn't much, but it was enough to get me back and forth to work. I would come to affectionately call it "Christine," after the car in the Stephen King novel, because it gradually developed a mind of its own.

Broadcasting the news every Saturday and Sunday night significantly cut into my drinking time. It was actually a good thing because it helped me party less and focus more on the future.

And there was still the issue of Marty. I was still procrastinating. At a small off-campus party on the first Friday after Thanksgiving break I met a friend of Marty's. I was nursing a beer when this girl sidled up to me.

"You're Ed Crockett, aren't you?"

"Yes, I am. What is your name?"

"I'm Lisa, I'm a friend of Marty's. We watch you on the news all the time."

I was skeptical. I had only been "on the news" a few weekends, so watching me all the time seemed like a stretch.

"Is Marty here?"

"No. But you should ask her out."

I stared at her for a second. And then blurted out, "Would she go?"

"Oh yeah, definitely, would you like me to set it up?"

She caught me off guard. All I could come up with was, "No thanks, I can do that myself."

Lisa vanished as quickly as she had appeared.

I panicked.

Did I just tell a good friend of Marty's that I was going to ask her out?

I had to do something, but at this point, there were only three weeks of classes left until Christmas break and luckily I didn't run into Martha. I wanted to ask her out, but I was *still* making excuses.

At home for Christmas, I visited my sister Gin on Sherwood Street in Portland and told her about Martha and how much I liked her. I conveyed my concern about starting something that would probably be over before it even got started because I was graduating. Gin straightened me out.

"Stop overthinking it. You don't know what graduation will bring, so don't assume the worst. Go with your heart and see what happens."

It was great advice. I needed to just do it.

Since I was working as the weekend anchor, I was locked into being in Bangor every Saturday and Sunday night, even during school break. The eleven o'clock news broadcast was truly a one-man show. It was just me and one production guy in the building. He pressed buttons for commercials, but for all intents and

This is Martha and me in the early '80s.

purposes he was nonexistent. I'd arrive around eight to start pulling stories together. Everything I read came off the Associated Press newswire. Occasionally, the six o'clock news crew would leave me a video or copy to re-air, or a touchy-feely feature that didn't make the six o'clock broadcast. I had to be on air at ten each night with a twenty-second teaser. I liked doing the tease, because twenty seconds of copy fit perfectly on the teleprompter. With one page my head could remain upright and steady while reading, unlike with the full newscast when my head would be bobbing up and down throughout. My production guy wanted nothing to do with operating the teleprompter.

The actual broadcast was supposed to be structured as follows: read national and local news (seven minutes), commercial break (one minute), sports (three minutes), commercial break (one minute), weather (two minutes), and then sign off. Reading the small wire copy was challenging but manageable once I was comfortable with it. No wire copy was needed to do the sports report, since I could ad lib or cut away to game feeds. That's what Frank Fixaris, the sports anchor at WGAN in Portland, did when I was an intern. Imitation is the sincerest form of flattery.

Every two weeks I met with Gordon Manuel to review recent broadcasts. These meetings were usually routine, so I wasn't concerned. I should have been. We were sitting in the editing booth on a Monday picking apart the previous evening's broadcast when he stopped the tape. He looked me in the eyes and barked, "Ed, this is a *newscast*, not a *sports* show."

I wasn't sure where he was going with this until he added, "You have twelve minutes of air time (not counting the commercials), and last night your sports segment lasted more than nine minutes. Please keep sports to three or four minutes."

After an awkward few seconds he smiled.

"You're doing a great job."

I was self-conscious about my head bobbing up and down while reading the news (sometimes I'd lose my place) and giving the weather (no maps). Meanwhile, ad libbing sports was easy; I could do it without a script. I don't think the audience minded, but his suggestion to bring balance to the newscast was the right one.

Even though I began to curtail my partying ways before taking the job at WABI, having to be professional until midnight on Saturday and Sunday nights was just what the doctor ordered. I also discovered that trying to catch up with my drunken friends was a fruitless task. I'd show up at midnight and think, "Oh god, is that how I look?" Although it wasn't pretty, I tried catching up a few times before realizing it was a waste of effort and energy. So, rather than guzzle to match their state, I chilled out and didn't feel shitty the next day.

Gin's talk finally convinced me to ask Martha out on a date. I was planning to call her once I was back at school, but as fate would have it we bumped into each other in Portland on New Year's Eve. I was out on the town with my Surplus Store buddies, and they mentioned a party at an old high school classmate's house. My friends were in the same class as Martha and her friend Renee who was hosting the party. The party was rocking with dozens of local kids. While making my way downstairs, I saw Martha coming up. I had no idea that she and Renee were friends and wasn't expecting to see her. I briefly froze, but quickly gathered myself and after some small talk, I *finally* asked her out. We made plans to connect at school, and just like that after four years of thinking about her, on New Year's Eve 1982, everything became clear.

Unexpectedly, I ran into Martha on campus before the semester started. On the last weekend before classes began, the Maine hockey team played a Friday night home game at Alfond Arena. I returned a day early to attend the game and then stayed to work over the weekend. Martha, who was a resident assistant, came back early and went to the game with her friend Dino. Dino, as I learned later, was the boyfriend of the girl, Lisa, who had approached me at the party back in November. Lisa thought Dino was spending too much time with Martha and decided getting Martha a boyfriend would put an end to the problem.

Since we were both busy on campus and a little apprehensive about starting a relationship, our courtship moved slowly. For the first three months or so we would go out maybe once or twice a week. It also soon became apparent that I was Martha's first real boyfriend. We enjoyed each other's company and grew closer and closer by the day.

My broadcasting the news on television added some amusement to our relationship. Martha tuned in occasionally, but a few of the younger girls on her floor watched closely and reported back to Martha about my performance. Their recap included any grammatical errors or flubbed words, but it mostly pertained to my fashion choices. Either my tie was ugly or didn't match the jacket, or my hair was a mess. It was entertaining and they had a good laugh at my expense.

Although we were dating, most friends and family inside and outside of Orono were not aware of our relationship. Eventually, Martha's parents got wind that she was dating, and wanted to meet her boyfriend. Although I now saw my father and Ann regularly, I hadn't introduced her to them. My dilemma was that I couldn't present Martha, the girl I was falling in love with, to them before I introduced her to my mother. It just didn't seem right. Of course, this may have been another excuse to keep my father at a distance, but I strongly believed my mother deserved to meet Martha first. Not doing it that way almost seemed disloyal. Since Ma didn't drive, she wasn't coming to Orono anytime soon, so I planned to introduce Martha to Ma when we were home for spring break in March. For the time being, I just needed to come up with fresh excuses why we couldn't go to my father's for dinner.

Once Martha's parents and siblings heard she had a boyfriend, she was bombarded with questions. Martha had three older siblings graduate from Maine, and her Uncle Dave was Dean of Students. I had actually met Dean Rand in passing, but I was still a mystery man to the family. Since Martha hadn't dated much, I was big news. Her parents, Bud and Pat, couldn't wait to meet her new beau. Apparently waiting for March break didn't fly, since Martha phoned me on a Wednesday night in late February and said, "My parents are coming to town Friday, and we have dinner plans at Baldacci's Restaurant."

Although I was excited about meeting her parents, I teased, "If they don't like me, at least I'll get a good meal." Baldacci's had the best Italian food around, and I loved Italian food. She ignored my lame attempt at humor.

Bud and Pat were great, warm and welcoming. I was much more anxious about Martha meeting Ma and seeing where I lived than meeting her parents. I was always embarrassed to bring anyone to 60 Kellogg Street, but it was the only way to meet Ma, since she wasn't coming to us. I prepped, no, I warned Martha about what to expect. She'd meet my mother and probably not get a word in edgewise. Ma could talk and was a terrible listener, so you were better off just nodding and being polite. I also wondered, "How do you prepare somebody for more than a dozen house pets, their hair everywhere, and the accompanying odor?" I did my best to make excuses, but ultimately I just told it like it was. And prayed.

The introduction went well because Martha, as always, was gracious and understanding. She sat on the clawed-up couch and we weren't there more than five minutes before she was swarmed by at least a half-dozen cats. They walked across her lap, rubbed against her body, settled in around her head, and sniffed her feet. She smiled and listened to Ma gab.

We did not stay long. I surely used some clever ruse to get her out of there quickly, which seemed the wisest course of action. The place, as always, was a disaster, only slightly less disheveled than when other humans regularly lived there. My brother Walt and sister Carolyn had both put 60 Kellogg in their rearview mirror. Walt was in the Army and Carolyn was married. It was now difficult for me to stay at the house even just during school vacations. Having been mostly away for four years, I found that my sinuses could no longer handle the pet overload anymore. I'd be in the house for a few minutes and my nose would plug and my eyes would redden. I had become allergic to cats and dogs. The human body is amazing. While living in that environment for over twenty years, my body coped, but when I left it screamed: "Enough is enough!"

Martha lived in the North Deering section of Portland, about five miles from Munjoy Hill. After leaving my mother's house I took her home. I was worried about the visit. I recalled what happened with Jeanne.

Martha, of course, relieved my concerns immediately.

She turned to me with a big smile.

"Jesus, you weren't kidding. There were cats in my face before my butt hit the cushion."

"I'm sorry."

She smiled and waved it off.

"Your mother is lovely."

This girl was the one.

Chapter Fourteen
Broadcast News

Now that Martha had met Ma, toward the end of the semester I brought her along to dinner at my father's place a few times. The conversation was always light and took my mind off more pressing matters, like finding a job.

During one of our visits I learned that one of my father's passions was music. Despite how he had treated his body, Walter could still sing, and he entertained us with songs from his youth. He wasn't up to date, seventeen years on the streets will do that I suppose, but he nailed songs from the '50s and '60s. Walter was a proud Irishman and an honorary Irish Rover (from the 1960s TV show, The Irish Rovers) who would belt out all the tunes. It was both entertaining and instructional, since I was unfamiliar with the songs. Listening to his brogue was amazing.

I, on the other hand, was not a music buff. In fact, as a child I had little interest in it. I enjoyed dancing and music provided pleasurable background noise, but I hardly noticed what the songs were. Before college the only music I listened to was Elvis Presley (Ma owned many of the King's albums) and American Top 40 on the radio. Fortunately Carolyn was an aficionado. She familiarized me with Carole King and Elton John, two artists who rank among my favorites. "Tapestry" by Carole King was the first non-Elvis album I ever heard, and "Elton John's Greatest Hits" soon followed. Carolyn began with ballads, then expanded my ear to rock 'n' roll with a crash course on bands like The Rolling Stones, Aerosmith, and The Cars to help cover my ignorance before I went to college.

Although Walter would have preferred a singer, he watched my newscasts religiously and was my biggest fan. He refused to go to bed on Saturday or Sunday nights until I signed off. That was fine on Saturday, but on Sunday he lost sleep since he had to be at Husson by seven. His feedback was appreciated. His loyalty was flattering.

My father occasionally asked my opinion on a variety of topics, even about himself. The latter was risky, because I had opinions and I spoke freely. This didn't always sit well, although he did appreciate my candor.

One night he asked, "Eddie, do you have a favorite song?"

I had one, but I hesitated to share it with him. My favorite song was a ballad, and I liked the story and the message—"Cat's in the Cradle" by Harry Chapin. The song about a shitty dad became my leitmotif. In the song, a young son wants to spend time with his father, but his father is always too busy. One verse, includes these lines:

> *When you coming home, dad?*
> *I don't know when,*
> *But we'll get together then*
> *You know we'll have a good time then*

The kicker to the song is that the young son always proclaims that he wants to be just like his dad. Finally, when the father has grown old and wants to see his son, the son now says he is too busy to visit the old man. The father realizes it has all come true.

I said, I'd like to see you if you don't mind
He said, I'd love to, dad, if I can find the time
You see, my new job's a hassle, and the kids have the flu
But it's sure nice talking to you, dad
It's been sure nice talking to you
And as I hung up the phone, it occurred to me
He'd grown up just like me
My boy was just like me

I promised myself that I would never become as shitty a dad to my kids. I would break the cycle. My song revelation tempered our conversation for the rest of the evening.

It was getting late in the college game, mid-April, and I had no job offers on the table when the phone rang at the fraternity house. It was the station manager, David Taylor, from WGAN, where I had interned. He was a wonderful mentor and was reaching out regarding a part-time position, news assignment editor, on his team. Since WABI didn't have such a role, I wasn't sure exactly what it entailed. Taylor summarized the responsibilities saying, "You will coordinate staff activities and assign reporters to that day's stories."

I thoroughly enjoyed my summer internship at Channel 13, and excitedly accepted his offer. Although it was only weekends, it was a job in my major, and being in Portland was comforting since, although not ideal, I could live at home rent-free. Of course, the big drawback was I didn't want to go back to Kellogg Street, in large part because I couldn't breathe. However, I felt getting my foot in the door at WGAN outweighed any breathing issues.

I shared the Portland news with Gordon Manuel at WABI. He congratulated me. But a week later during our regular weekly review he offered me a full-time news assignment editor position.

Apparently, he had been considering adding such a role to his team and my job offer in Portland highlighted the need for a similar role at WABI. I had done well anchoring the weekend news, mainly being dependable and prompt, so he gave me my first hard sell. He expounded on how hard it is to break into the broadcasting business, and kept hammering that the job was full-time. Excited and confused, I called David Taylor and told him about my new opportunity. He advised me to take the full-time position, and said he would keep me in mind if something full-time developed at WGAN. Sorrowfully, David soon got terrible news; he was diagnosed with cancer and would die within months. I learned about his death by reading his obituary. I've often wondered if my career would have turned out differently if I'd taken that part-time job and gotten my foot in the door in Portland. David was a true professional, an unselfish leader who gave me sound advice. He was a great man and mentor.

I graduated from the University of Maine in May 1983 and immediately began working full-time at Channel 5. I was one of only five broadcast journalism students employed full-time in radio or television upon graduation. Maine was not known for producing broadcast journalists; I was fortunate to have a job in the industry. The fact that it paid only $10,400 a year didn't faze me (at least until I went apartment hunting). I was doing something I liked and working in my chosen field. Plus, I was in love with Martha, so staying around Orono for her senior year was auspicious.

Apartments in and around Bangor were not expensive, but I couldn't afford one. A friend of the family, Peter Millard, his wife, Emily, and young son Cameron, had a house in Orono and offered me a room. The Millards were hip folks. They welcomed me into their home like I was one of their own. My simple dream of being independent was realized. I had graduated, found a full-time job, and wasn't living at 60 Kellogg Street. I was feeling good, but didn't really have a long-term plan. It was my love of sports that drew me into broadcasting and it was working out.

I was told that you go to college to prepare yourself for the real world. At least that was the bill of goods I was sold. You're charged with going four or more years in this environment with no real responsibilities other than to get passing grades and graduate. Does this prepare you for the "real world" of forty-plus-hour weeks with early mornings and late nights? Of course not. College is the bridge to responsibility. Hopefully, it gives you time to mature and get somewhat prepared for the nine-to-five grind. I quickly realized that this job thing was intense, unforgiving, and downright scary. Skipping a few eight o'clock classes in college wasn't a problem, but if I was a few minutes late for work, there'd be hell to pay.

I had never been a full-time salaried employee, but it didn't take long to understand what it meant. Forty hour weeks, yeah right, try fifty plus most weeks and often times north of sixty. Didn't matter how many hours, the paycheck still said two hundred dollars, and that was before taxes.

The real-world grind was exhausting. Luckily, I worked with talented people who broke me in slowly. I enjoyed anchoring, but soon realized it wasn't my passion. I discovered that if one is meant for the broadcast news business, the rush of being on air remains constant. Initially I felt being on TV was cool. Fellow students recognized me and passed along complimentary words, while total strangers stopped me at the mall and said hello. Although I had some shortcomings, most notably a thick Maine accent and little interest in non-sports news, I thought I'd make a good broadcaster. In the end, I didn't love it. So when the assignment editor opportunity showed itself, I was genuinely excited about learning another aspect of broadcast journalism.

Commencing work right after graduation was ideal. I needed the money and with all of my friends from school gone home or starting their careers elsewhere, Orono was a ghost town. The solitude cut my socializing and drinking time down to zero. Even if there had been friends around, I doubt I would have partied much, since I was sleeping in a room adjacent to a two-year-old. Even I knew coming in shit-faced would not have gone over well, and being hungover at school was different from being hungover at work. As it turned out I didn't even have my father and Ann around to grab the occasional home-cooked meal. Ann had finished up her master's work, and they moved back to Portland that June. I wouldn't see them again until the holidays.

Although work was going well, six months in I began questioning my career choice. I still had occasional thoughts about being a sports broadcaster, but the rush was gone. I put together demo tapes so I could send them to stations across the country but I never mailed them. My heart wasn't in it. However, as assignment editor I was learning the business side of the operation and was enjoying it. Following long conversations with Martha, and feelers with some family and friends, it was obvious my interests were more behind the scenes than in front of the camera. So after weighing my options I decided to pursue a Master's of Business Administration.

My changing interests were the primary motivators for the move, but I'd be lying if I said money wasn't a factor. Television broadcasting is a glamorous profession; after all, everybody sees your face on the screen. As a result the candidate pool, especially in the smaller markets, is much greater than the demand. Stations can pay low wages for your services. The MBA brochures declared graduates were demanding salaries north of fifty thousand dollars to start, with a variety of perks. That definitely appealed to me. I applied to three schools: Maine, Boston University, and Boston

College. Maine was my safety school. I was confident that I'd get admitted, but I had my heart set on the two Boston schools. BC was my first choice. BU was ranked higher than BC in *Business Week*, but BC's program was young, small, and coming on strong. Plus, they had Division I basketball and football programs, and I wanted to spend my two years of school in that atmosphere. I heard from BU first, and they accepted me into the class of 1986. I didn't hear from Boston College until April and I was wait-listed.

"Wait-listed, what the hell is that?" I exclaimed. I understood that I wasn't rejected, but it didn't sound like I was still being considered, either.

I called the Carroll Graduate School of Management office asking for clarification, and the receptionist told me: "It means we are keeping your application open pending the matriculation of accepted students."

Like so many things, it was a numbers game. In this case the program had ninety spots for incoming first years, and they sent out a few hundred acceptance letters hoping at least ninety would accept and enroll. They built a waitlist in case the number of students who accepted the offer was lower than expected. If that happens, they go down the wait list to fill the open slots. My naiveté proved helpful here. I didn't know how the system worked and never got down about it. Instead, I moved into sales mode. I felt a face to face meeting would serve me well, so I requested an interview to discuss my application and status. The school promptly denied my request saying they did not grant interviews to any applicants. They did leave a crack though; I could check in periodically on the status of my application.

Since I had been accepted at Maine and BU, I knew my time at WABI was short. I resigned from my position in May 1984 shortly after Martha's graduation. Martha was going back to work at Johnny's Oarweed Restaurant in Ogunquit, where she had worked every summer since high school as a waitress and hostess. Johnny's Oarweed was a checkered tablecloth establishment in Perkins Cove, sitting on the water at the end of the majestic Marginal Way. It was arguably the most popular restaurant in town.

I decided to follow Martha to Ogunquit. A good friend and fellow broadcast journalism graduate from Maine, Brad, lived in Ogunquit and worked as a cook at Gypsy Sweethearts restaurant. He told me the owners were looking for a service bartender to work breakfast and dinner, and he offered me a cheap room at his place. Ogunquit is, in my opinion, the most beautiful spot in Maine. It is a tiny town often referred to as the "Provincetown of Maine" since it is a popular destination for gay tourists. The beach is famous, and the nightlife is active with restaurants, theatres, and clubs.

Every two weeks, I called Boston College asking for a personal interview. Each time I was turned away. Finally, on a Friday morning in late May, the director of admissions relented and invited me down to review my application the following Monday morning. I was excited, but I did not want to get my hopes up. My car, Christine, was in the shop and the bus would not get me to BC in time. Once again my brother-in-law Bruce came to the rescue. His wholesale food company made daily runs to Boston, so I jumped on one of his trucks, and got dropped off at the train station. From there, I took the subway to the BC campus. The Green Line conveniently ended on Commonwealth Avenue directly across from the Boston College entrance. At the time this all seemed very normal to me. You jumped through whatever hoops were necessary to make it work.

The interview went well, and within a week my wait-listed status was upgraded to "accepted."

I was taking my talents to Chestnut Hill.

Chapter Fifteen
Boston College

Graduate school was expensive, about $35,000 a year. I received maximum assistance, which was key, but I still had to take out large loans. Assuming I found cheap housing and scored a part-time job, the sticker price would be manageable. In early August, I traveled to Boston College to check out apartments, dragging my friend Brad along with me. My plan, mapped out at the last minute in the Gypsy Sweethearts bar with Martha and Brad, was to find an apartment, meet up with my brother Jimmy and his fiancée, Anna, who were living in Southie, and then go see a James Taylor concert on the Boston Common.

Martha was not impressed.

"What kind of plan is that? You expect to find a place to live in a couple hours?"

"How hard can it be to find a room?"

Martha shook her head and turned to Brad.

"Brad, just a word to the wise. Jimmy is a wild man. Please don't do anything stupid."

The campus housing office suggested I connect with other incoming students. I met two guys and we looked at a couple of places, including this fantastic, spacious apartment just a few blocks from campus. I really wanted it, but it was well beyond my budget.

At Jimmy and Anna's, my brother inquired, "So, how did the apartment search go?"

"We saw this great place right near campus, but it was way too rich. I think it's going to work out for some classmates though. I signed a lease with two other guys, but they'll need to pull somebody else in. It sucks because the place is really nice and convenient. But it's a grand a month and I can only afford a few hundred. I'm going to have to look a bit farther away."

"Let's look at places in Brighton in the morning," Jimmy said. "I used to live there. It won't be as nice, but it will be more affordable."

"That would be great." I rolled my eyes and sarcastically added, "No biggie, plenty of time. School only starts in a month."

Jimmy placed full shot glasses in front of us.

"What are we shooting here? It smells like licorice," Brad said.

"It's sambuca, the Greek god of liquor. Throw it back quickly, it's real smooth."

Shots of sambuca kicked off an unforgettable night in Boston with my brother. Well, memorable for some of us anyway. Following shots at Jimmy's place, the three of us drove to the Purple Shamrock at Quincy Market. Jimmy continued to set us up with shots of sambuca and pints of Guinness.

The James Taylor concert was awesome, but the aftermath was regrettable. We just drank so much. When we got back to Southie, Brad got sick. I remember sitting out on the patio nursing him, but that is the last thing I remembered. I woke up the next morning on the couch. Anna was sitting in the kitchen enjoying a cup of coffee.

I stumbled over.

"Good morning, where is everybody?"

"Jimmy's in bed and your friend Brad is still out on the patio."

"Brad is still outside?"

"I got you to come in around three, but we couldn't move him."

"Holy shit, is it safe?"

"Yeah. The patio is gated. I brought him some covers and a pillow. Go check for yourself."

I checked on Brad and then thanked Anna.

"You guys got way out of hand. It was fortunate you got back here at all."

"I remember Brad getting sick walking back, but not much else."

"Jimmy got you home. Brad got sick as soon as Jimmy parked the car. Good thing he made it to the sidewalk. I wouldn't have been happy if he'd lost it in the car."

"How did Brad end up out on the patio?"

"You and Jimmy dragged him inside the gate; he just wanted to lie down. You stayed with him for about an hour, before passing out. How are you feeling?"

"Terrible."

I was embarrassed. I apologized to my future sister-in-law. And I asked myself, "Am I ever going to grow up?"

My father's fate was never far from my mind nor was Ma's assertion that it only takes one drink to become an alcoholic. I could still hear her constant refrain: "If you drink, you will be just like your father: living on the streets."

It turns out my mother was wrong. And my father's issues were his own.

That night in Boston was my final wake-up call. Not that the fear of alcoholism was fully conquered, but never again would I drink to the point of blacking out. I was lucky, I guess. If there really was an "alcoholic gene" in the family, as my mother always said, it may have bit my father, my uncles, and my grandfather, but it seemed to have just nibbled at me.

After having witnessed so much alcohol abuse in my family and on Munjoy Hill, I'm convinced that alcohol addiction is a hereditary trait that is also exacerbated by the social environment. If you play with this fire, eventually you will get burned. I count my blessings often, because I foolishly tested Ma's theory and ignored the history of my gene pool and my neighborhood.

Chestnut Hill was not Munjoy Hill and graduate school required huge adjustments. I was once again flat broke, and immediately doubted I could make the cut in graduate school. I was a good student, but I constantly wondered, "Am I in over my head here?"

Boston was not Bangor or Portland, and trying to navigate the city was overwhelming. I felt isolated and alone. I was living with strangers in an apartment only slightly more appealing than 60 Kellogg Street. Once again, my self-confidence was shaken.

My fears grew more acute following my first accounting exam. I prepared and thought I did well. But a week later the professor returned the exam and announced, "This easy test will be your one gift this semester."

The class average was 96. I got an 80. My confidence was shattered.

I cried myself to sleep that night. And I am not ashamed to say, I cried myself to sleep a few more nights that semester.

My only saving grace was Martha Rand.

Martha lived at home in Portland working for Carroll Reed, a clothing store located downtown. Thankfully, she bought a white Mazda GLC hatchback and drove down to visit me every other weekend. She lifted my spirits each time, and then I'd hang on as best I could until her next visit.

Before the next accounting exam, the professor made it clear this test would not be as easy as the first. I again put in ample study time, but I went into the test timidly. It was a long week waiting for the results. The class average was 78. I got a 95. It was worth the wait.

The sports at Boston College didn't disappoint. The basketball team was coming into its own with guards like Michael Adams and Dana Barros. BC played in the newly formed Big East Conference, perhaps the best basketball league in college history. The Big East meant BC played Georgetown with Patrick Ewing, St. John's with Chris Mullin, Villanova with Ed Pinckney, and Syracuse with Pearl Washington. When the big-name teams came to town they played at the old Boston Garden. I went to as many games as possible and got to see BC upset Pearl Washington and Syracuse.

A much bigger deal in BC Nation was Doug Flutie. My first year at Boston College coincided with Flutie's senior football season. I was perhaps fortunate to have applied to BC before Flutie mania set in. In the wake of Flutie's legendary Hail Mary pass to Gerard Phelan that stunned the Miami Hurricanes in November 1984, applications to BC skyrocketed. Doug Flutie was a five-foot88t, nine-inches tall (at best), scrambling quarterback from nearby Natick. He led BC to a top five national ranking, and won the Heisman Trophy, which is given to the nation's best college player each year.

One last note on Doug Flutie. Although we never formally met, I did play pick-up basketball with him in the field house, and he left a lasting impression. I was dribbling downcourt and threw an ill-advised cross-court pass when out of nowhere this flash

My Boston College graduation photo in 1986.

picked off my pass, raced downcourt, and slammed it through the hoop. Everybody's jaw just dropped. Of course, we had all heard the legend of this amazing athlete, but I had a hard time believing this guy at least three inches shorter than me could dunk a basketball. I couldn't even touch the rim, so to see him dunk, no, smash it through the hoop with authority, was awesome. Rumor had it he could have walked onto the basketball team and contributed. I believe it.

In December 1984, I promised Martha that we would be engaged by her birthday on March 11. We had talked about getting married, so my declaration wasn't startling. But it did mean that I was now on the clock. I had only three months to propose and a lot to do. First, I wanted to buy an engagement ring. Second, I still wanted the proposal to be somewhat of a surprise. Third, I wanted to ask Bud and Pat for their blessing.

Martha wasn't a jewelry person; in fact her ears have never been pierced. About the only jewelry she wore was a watch. Still, I needed to get a ring. A BC friend, Kathy, offered to help out. Her offer was huge since, like most things when it came to women, I was clueless. Kathy and I started the ring search in Boston's diamond district. Predictably my dreams didn't match my budget. I had loans to cover my tuition and housing, and a part-time job at a college sub shop to buy food and have a little spending money. But I was naïve thinking about what kind of ring I could get for a few hundred dollars. I found out that not many nice diamonds go for two hundred bucks. I quickly got discouraged. Kathy finally took me to Filene's Basement where I found a ½-karat sapphire with a tiny diamond on each side in my price range.

I assumed Martha was expecting a formal proposal on a major holiday—Christmas, New Year's, and Valentine's Day were all before my self-imposed March 11 deadline. Although I'm not the most creative guy, even I understood that proposing on a holiday was too predictable. What to do? I decided to propose on my mother's birthday. Yes, this was almost as much for my mother as it was to catch Martha off guard. Ma's birthday was February 17. The timing was perfect, since it fell between Valentine's Day and Martha's birthday in March. I figured once we got past Valentine's Day, Martha would assume the proposal was planned for her birthday.

Valentine's Day in 1985 was on a Thursday. I drove to Portland and Martha and I celebrated the evening together. There was no proposal. Although she never mentioned it, Martha probably pondered, "What the hell is he waiting for?"

While in town, I met with Bud and Pat to ask their permission to marry their daughter. That part was easy, since everyone including Bud and Pat assumed it was just a matter of time. I was a little worried, because Bud could be a practical joker and might make me sweat. He didn't.

That Sunday night, I took Martha and my mother to dinner in the Old Port. Since it was my mother's birthday, I figured Martha would not suspect a proposal was in the works. I chose a Chinese restaurant on Brown Street because we all liked Chinese food, and it fit into my master scheme. I had pre-printed my proposal—"Martha, will you marry me"—on a white strip of paper that would fit inside a fortune cookie. I went to the restaurant to discuss my plan and a waitress agreed to slip the proposal into Martha's fortune cookie. She would give the cookie to Martha at the end of our meal. And I'd also have the ring with me.

I was correct. Martha was totally caught off guard by the note in her fortune cookie. She recovered quickly though and said, "Yes."

Ma was bawling.

She was honored to be on hand and, for one of the few times in her life, was speechless. I loved my mother and thought it would be cool for her to be there. She had sacrificed everything for me, and I knew she would enjoy this twist on her birthday.

I called my father the following day.

He was delighted and added, "What took you so long?"

It was all good, but as it had my entire life, a lack of money once again reared its ugly head. While preparing for my second semester at Boston College I realized I didn't have enough money to pay all the bills. I wanted to do the right thing, so I stopped by the graduate school office and asked for a meeting with the dean. To my surprise Dean Torbert was on sabbatical and Dean Lewis, an interim dean, was in charge.

"Ed, what can I do for you?"

"Dean Lewis, I'm going to have to drop one of my classes, because I don't have enough money to pay for it. Which class would you recommend I drop that won't slow advancement toward my degree?"

He was silent. He looked at me and said, "Give me a minute."

I watched as he opened a file on the computer, but it was difficult to see. Putting on my glasses for a closer look would have helped, but I didn't want to come off as intrusive. He turned in his chair, faced me, and said, "Come back and see me a week from today."

"Should I stop attending one of my classes?"

"No, go to all your classes. I'll see you next week."

The meeting left me perplexed, but I returned the following week. Dean Lewis opened the meeting with news that the 1984-85 school year marked the twenty-fifth anniversary of the Boston College MBA program. He was coordinating a celebration, scheduled for April 1985, and asked if I'd be interested in an internship to work on the project. He valued the internship at the same dollar rate as one class. I accepted and remained on course for graduation. In that previous meeting, Dean Lewis had pulled up my first semester transcript on the computer. Thankfully, I had done well, and that gave him enough pause to consider how to help. He also stated his respect toward my approach. I wasn't asking for anything, just looking for advice.

This opportunity proved to be a big break. I was assigned to work with Dean Lewis' staff, particularly his secretaries Priscilla and Ann, as well as the director of admissions with whom I had interviewed months earlier. Although the job—pulling addresses, mailing letters, making phone calls—was uninspiring, the company was fun. Priscilla and Ann were wonderful, both around my mother's age, and we hit it off instantly. I spent as much time talking and joking with them as I did working. They learned my story, could relate, and were incredibly supportive.

However, even with the internship, my money dried up in April. I was flat broke and I couldn't pay my rent for May.

Fortunately, Jimmy and Anna now only lived about a mile away, so they were there to save the day. On April 30, I moved all my belongings into Christine and crashed on Jimmy's couch through finals.

Chapter Sixteen
Family Business

The money issue was not going away.

Returning to Portland for the summer of 1985 was a given, after all Martha, now my fiancée, was there. Still I was edgy with my living arrangements up in the air. Of course, Ma always welcomed me back. I could have squatted at 60 Kellogg Street, but not being able to breathe ruled that out and I couldn't afford to rent an apartment. Once again, the family stepped up. My brother David and his wife, Mel, who had recently relocated to North Deering, offered me refuge. The only available space in their home was an alcove adjacent to the garage. But hey, I was moving on up. At least I wouldn't be living out of the car.

The accommodations proved better than initially presented. The alcove, which jutted off the side of the one-car garage, had enough room to fit a twin bed, nightstand, and chest of drawers, and the nook was private with its own entry door. As an added bonus, Martha's parents' house was only a half-mile away. I can only imagine what my future in-laws thought of this arrangement—their future son-in-law was in a fiscal crisis, unsure about how to pay for graduate school, unemployed, and living in his brother's garage. Thank God they had rose-colored glasses.

Before leaving Boston College in May, I declared marketing as my concentration and I chose my fall classes. My attitude was a bit negative because it seemed unlikely I could afford to return to the Heights for my second year in September. My only chance of continuing as a full-time student was to nab one of the three assistantships offered through the Carroll School of Management office. These assistantships waived tuition and provided a healthy stipend.

The three assistantships available were: Assistant to the Dean, Assistant to the Director of Career Placement, and Assistant to the Director of Admissions. I didn't have any shot at the first one because it was reserved for a top-ranked student only. My grades were in the top twenty, but not in the required top five. That left two director positions as viable options. However, I didn't know anyone at the career placement office and with my limited professional work experience, I probably wasn't the strongest candidate. That left the admissions position as my only realistic hope. The good news was that I knew the admissions team well because I worked closely with them on the twenty-fifth anniversary project. There was hope.

Returning home in May, not knowing if I'd be able to go back to school in the fall was unsettling. I started to mentally prepare myself to go to work, build some savings, and then finish my MBA as a part-time student. That wasn't my original plan, but it seemed like the only reasonable option at that moment.

By the summer of 1985, my father had started his own painting business. Word on the street was that he was both talented and efficient. It seemed surprising, perhaps shocking to me, considering all the time he spent on the streets, but he still had dozens of friends and acquaintances around Greater Portland who were willing and ready to hire him. After Walter and Ann returned from

My dad and his second wife, Ann, with Martha and me on our wedding day in June 1986.

Orono, he took a lot of odd jobs, working consistently and saving enough money to invest in a truck and all the equipment he needed to venture out on his own as a professional painter.

When I was home in February, he offered me a job working on his crew. He didn't need me, but he was hopeful that I'd accept. I left him hanging for a bit, although that was not my intention. I was excited, but hesitant.

Was working for my father a good idea?

I truly didn't know. I definitely had not forgiven him for abandoning us, and it wasn't like he was offering me big bucks. It was a minimum-wage job, and I had been hoping for something more lucrative. He knew I was reluctant to commit, so he did not attempt to force the issue. He let it come, slowly. Since nothing better developed, I decided to spend the summer working for my father. In truth, I didn't look that hard.

The summer emerged as a milestone in our relationship. I don't believe I would have ever given him the chance to know me, and vice versa, if I hadn't accepted his offer. Yes, a marketing job or internship would have been the more career-oriented route, but this was personal and, in the grand scheme, considerably more important. My father deserves all the credit for trying to re-establish contact. I would have kept him at a distance. Working together each day did not solve all of our problems, but it changed our lives. Although he was guarded too, he gradually opened up. We spent most days on the job talking about my plans. He didn't really grasp the whole career thing; he was more about how hard work earns good pay. His work ethic was contagious, and it was easy to see why so many friends kept giving him a chance. He was one hell of a worker, fast and first-rate. We spent that summer working on two big jobs. The first was a commercial office building near the hospital that required an indoor overhaul. There were twenty or so offices that needed a fresh coat of paint, and most were a lackluster cream shade. The second job was an impressive spread that included a horse barn in North Deering. Both jobs took several weeks, giving us plenty of time to bond.

I was a good painter, but slow as molasses. I was meticulous in an environment that demanded speed. His patience was extraordinary. Without question I slowed him down, but he never complained or rushed me. He was just happy to be sober and spending time with his youngest son. By this point, Walter had been dry for five years and was gaining confidence in his ability to stay sober. Even so, he understood he was one drink away from losing everything again. Walter and Ann lived in an apartment off Forest Avenue on the outskirts of Portland, miles from his old stomping grounds. His family was nearby. Walt had returned from the Army and settled in Maine, and Carolyn lived locally, too. Having all this family around was a godsend, since we all kept them, especially Walter, busy. Walter's biggest fear, regarding a relapse, was boredom.

"Too much time on my hands is not a good thing for me."

He needed to stay active and keep his mind on the present. Martha and I spent many nights visiting Walter and Ann that summer. We'd usually have dinner then play a game of Trivial Pursuit. Playing Trivial Pursuit against them was humbling. Ann was incredibly bright, so it came as no surprise when she answered every question correctly. She really did, so it goes without saying that we didn't win much. The real shocker was my father. The guy with an eighth-grade education was a renaissance man. He answered every music question and most of the science and English literature ones correctly.

On numerous occasions I asked him, "How the hell do you know all about Shakespeare or Chaucer?"

"I'm a trivia savant."

They kicked our butts. At least they were nice about it. That was probably a good thing, because if they'd been cocky I don't think we would have handled it as well. We were competitive and wanted to win.

The summer was wonderful, except for the nagging question: "Are you going back to school in the fall?" Finally, a letter from BC arrived offering me an interview for the assistant director of admissions position after the Fourth of July.

The interview ended up being more a meet-and-greet than job specific. Thanks to Priscilla and Ann, the new director was well aware of me and my skill set, so the conversation was relaxed. The position called for the candidate to attend seminars in the Northeast for recruiting purposes. Opting to concentrate in marketing and sales unwittingly made me an even stronger candidate for the role. I learned later that the assistantship was actually mine to lose, since Priscilla and Ann had already sold the new director on me. I left the meeting confident in my chances, but when a few weeks passed with no word from BC, panic was setting in. Finally on my birthday, July 31, the director called to offer me the assistantship. That birthday ranks up there as one of my best ever. I spent the day working beside my father; had a dinner date with my fiancée; and got word that my MBA plan was back on course.

In August, I headed to Boston to find an apartment. As luck would have it, the classmate who secured the assistant of career placement position, Dave, also needed housing. We met with a counselor at the housing office who gave us a lead on a place in Newton Center. The owner wanted two graduate students, preferably female, to live in her home while she was away for the year. She agreed to meet with us, but not before the counselor vouched for our character. The house was amazing. It had three floors with five bedrooms and three bathrooms. It was fully furnished. There was a long driveway and garage for ample off-street parking. The neighborhood was breathtaking, lined with similarly stately residences framed by majestic maple trees, and only two miles from campus. This most decidedly *was not* 60 Kellogg Street. The rent was ridiculously low for what we were getting. The owner just wanted two responsible adults who would respect and take care of the property. After touring the house, and looking at Dave for confirmation, I said, "We'll take it, if you'll have us." She shook our hands and the search for housing was over.

Even with the low rent and the stipend, I still needed more money to cover expenses. My only asset was my car, dear Christine. I sold it for roughly the same amount I had purchased it for three years earlier; shocking considering all the headaches it gave me. Lack of wheels wouldn't be a problem at school, because I had a bicycle and Dave had a car. Unlike my first year when I was required to take six classes a semester, only four classes were needed per term in my second year, and all in your chosen concentration, making the academics less stressful. Since I was also working fifteen to twenty hours each week at the assistantship position, fewer classes were a blessing.

As Martha and I planned our wedding, getting together as often as possible was a priority. Due to my schedule (most of my assistantship work was on Saturday and Sunday) Martha drove to Boston nearly every weekend. I finally got back home for an extended period during winter break, and it was hectic. The wedding was scheduled for June 21, 1986. We bounced between our parents' homes finalizing the plans. Although it was a blur, we did slow down enough to start a lovely Christmas tradition with my father and Ann. Ann was meticulous about her decorations, especially the tree. It was beautifully decorated with garland, ribbons, and trinkets, yet the most spellbinding aspect of her tree was its more than one hundred ornaments. Since the branches were literally covered with decorations, I had to look deep into the tree before realizing it was an imitation. Rather than buy a traditional balsam fir, Ann preferred an artificial one. The dimensions always remained the same, and she knew exactly where to place all the trimmings. If she hadn't told me, I wouldn't have known it was a fake. Martha suggested we add a decoration to their tree annually that would be of special sentiment to us all. That Christmas we gave them a Trivial Pursuit ornament. It brought big smiles and tears.

The final semester at Boston College went by quickly. The assistantship demanded considerably less of my time, since most of the forums and travel had taken place in the fall. It was time to focus on finding a career, or at least a position that could lead to a career. Not fully understanding the job-search process, I signed up for interviews with companies visiting campus. I had interest in brand management, but questioned my qualifications and experience for such roles. For example, Gillette arrived to interview candidates for product management positions. Having moved through the initial screening process, I received a call to meet at world headquarters in South Boston. I prepared what I thought was necessary, but soon realized I was in way over my head. The interviewer asked me questions about her brands and advertising strategies, and I bumbled my way through. My chance for a second interview was long gone before this conversation concluded. My answers lacked substance or imagination, and I didn't prepare any questions for her. The experience taught me a great deal and aided me going forward.

I was interested in pursuing a career in sales, but there weren't any postings targeting sales representatives in the career placement office. The MBA curriculum prepared students for brand and product management jobs, and companies came in droves looking to fill those roles. However, most organizations wanted graduates with more work experience.

The Brown-Forman Corporation, a distiller from Louisville that included Jack Daniel's and Southern Comfort in its portfolio, was the lone business targeting MBAs for sales and merchandising positions. Basically, these were entry-level jobs more often posted to undergrads where one learned the industry by placing displays of the company's products in liquor stores. Not very glamorous, but it offered a path to sales management or brand management if preferred. I was convinced that due to my limited experience, landing a prestigious brand management position that paid handsomely was unlikely. And with the wedding in two months, I felt pressure to be employed.

Full disclosure, the Brown-Forman position was the only hard offer I'd received, so I took it. Somehow, despite my family history, I didn't see the irony or danger of working for a liquor company.

June 21, 1986 was a perfect wedding day.

The temperature was close to ninety degrees under a cloudless sky. We were married at State Street Congregational Church in Portland. The wedding party was a family affair. At least one member of each of our siblings' families had a role in the service. Walt was the best man and Carolyn's children served as our ring bearer and flower girl. Martha took my breath away. I kept pinching myself to make sure this wasn't a dream.

My father was beaming with joy. Since he was present at Walt's wedding a few years earlier, this wasn't the first time he was around the family. Walter had become a standard fixture at his grandchildren's birthday parties and other family celebrations, and all welcomed him with open arms. He was always respectful to Ma and the family. To be honest, I sometimes thought he was too conscientious, often blending deep into the scenery, hesitant to interact.

There is a photo of Walter and Ma at our wedding reception that is hilarious. I asked them to be introduced together, and they appeared fine with it. But if a picture is truly worth a thousand words then you would have thought these two hated each other. Just before being announced the photographer snapped them

My parents on our wedding day. They don't look thrilled!

standing beside each other looking away with disdain. Ma's arm was cocked like it's pushing Walter away and the expressions on their faces were priceless. I chuckle every time I see the photo, because I'm sure there was a time when the looks would have been real and it wouldn't have been funny. On this day my mother and father were happy. The photo reminded me of another Ma-ism: "Believe none of what you hear and half of what you see."

We took our vows in the morning, which was fortuitous because Martha may have reconsidered based on my behavior the rest of the day. I wasn't boorish, I just didn't stop drinking. I actually thought I'd scored some points during the reception, since I resisted the urge to follow my brothers and many friends to the adjacent restaurant bar to watch the Boston Celtics take down the

Houston Rockets in the NBA Finals. I do remember Randy dragging me to the bar for shots of Jack Daniel's and my buddy, Bruce, handing me a beer to guzzle when "Hit Me with Your Best Shot" was played by the DJ.

After the reception, our wedding party and friends headed to Bruno's Restaurant on India Street. The Napolitano family owned Bruno's and one of the sons, Patsy, is my godfather. We arrived at Bruno's around six and left at closing time. I don't recall ever getting up from my seat on the deck, and there was always a drink in front of me. It was constant, and that was the problem. While sitting in Bruno's having a great time with my bride and friends, I didn't realize how shit-faced I had become.

A friend would stop by our table and say, "Noticed your rum and coke was getting low, here's another."

This went on for hours.

We were spending the night at a hotel about five miles from Bruno's before embarking on our honeymoon the next day. As soon as I lifted my ass out of the chair I knew I was in trouble. Staggering, I made it to the car fine, but couldn't drive. Fortunately, Martha was sober.

About a mile into our ride, I made my new bride pull off the road so I could puke. Lovely. I rode the rest of the way to the hotel with my head hanging out the window.

I was so drunk, she had to drag me to the room. It clearly was not the wedding night she had dreamed about.

I can't blame that one on my father, it was all on me.

Sorry, babe.

Chapter Seventeen
Those Damn Red Sox

The one thing my father and I always shared was a love of baseball.

At the end of every college baseball season the top eight Division I teams in the country meet at Rosenblatt Stadium in Omaha, Nebraska to determine the national champion. It is a double elimination tournament. In June 1986, the University of Maine advanced to its fifth College World Series in six years. This run coincided with my sophomore to senior years at Maine and for the final two years I was the student voice of Maine baseball. It was an exciting time, and I was able to enjoy most of it with my father, a huge baseball fan. Two years earlier, Maine finished third in the College World Series led by two future major league pitchers, Joe Johnson and Billy Swift. The 1986 team was led by a flamethrower named Scott Morse. Game 1 matched Maine against Arizona. By now Walter and Ann had purchased a home in the Portland suburb of Scarborough. I went there to enjoy the game with him. Watching baseball with my father was curative. We both loved the game, appreciated its nuances and strategies; and would commentate throughout the contest. In those moments I appreciated what I'd missed as a child.

Morse started the Arizona game. Through seven innings he shut out the powerful Wildcats while Maine's offense drove across seven runs. Up 7-0 going to the bottom of the eighth inning, Coach Winkin decided to pull Morse and save his arm for another day. As the call went out to the bullpen, Walter hemmed and hawed: "Wait a minute, why is he pulling that kid?"

"Winkin is saving him for Game 3. We win this one and he gets plenty of rest to come back. By pulling him now he'll be fresh for his next start. It's risky, but our bullpen has been lights out and we are up by seven. I like the move."

Walter nodded.

Our mood changed quickly.

Winkin turned to his closer to finish off the Wildcats. He got through the eighth inning, but not before surrendering four runs. We now had a pit in our stomachs. Maine failed to score in the top of the ninth inning. Winkin sent his closer back out to start the bottom half. All was still good; we had a three-run lead and our stopper looked strong. Before we knew it Arizona had loaded the bases. Winkin was on the mound pointing to his bullpen. He called on a spot starter and long reliever to save the day. To this day I feel sorry for that kid. With two outs and the bases loaded an Arizona batter ripped a ball into the Omaha night for a grand slam. It was over in that instant, Arizona won 8-7. Maine quietly exited the tournament in its next game, denying Morse the opportunity to pitch again. Arizona went on to win the 1986 College World Series.

Watching Maine collapse in such shocking fashion was nothing compared to what came next—the 1986 World Series. By that time, it had been nearly seventy years since the Red Sox had won a championship, and a growing contigent of fans, including Walter, blamed the drought on the Curse of the Bambino. Babe Ruth, perhaps the greatest baseball player in history, came up with the

Boston Red Sox in 1914 as an ace pitcher and prolific slugger. Shortly after winning the 1918 World Series the Red Sox sold him to the New York Yankees, where he helped win championships in the Bronx. The Sox had not won since then, and often lost in excruciating fashion.

The Red Sox were leading the New York Mets 3 games to 2 at the start of Game 6. As I have already mentioned, dramatic Red Sox losses in 1967, 1975, and 1978 led to excessive drinking and my father knocking on death's door. A World Series championship now, the team's first since 1918 would be truly cathartic and make sobriety that much sweeter.

Walter was sitting in his comfy chair sporting Red Sox apparel (a Yaz shirt and Sox cap) grinning ear to ear entering the ninth inning with the Sox leading. Sixty-eight years of futility would be erased in the next twenty minutes, and Walter could not have been happier. Redemption was on the doorstep. Sox reliever Calvin Schiraldi, who had been nearly unhittable in the second half of the season, was coming in to shut the door on the New York Mets.

The ninth inning was devastating.

When Mookie Wilson's ground ball scooted through Bill Buckner's legs allowing Ray Knight to score the winning run, my father was crushed. I was relieved he wasn't alone that evening, because high-stress emotional moments like that can result in irrational decisions which prove hazardous to one's health. If anything could have rocked his world into a relapse, it would be a Boston Red Sox loss, which, after all, was at the root of three of his five brushes with death. Watching him suffer through that Game 6 loss was brutal.

We were silent listening to Hall of Fame Broadcaster Vin Scully make the call, "So the winning run is at second base, with two outs, three and two to Mookie Wilson. (A) Little roller up along first... behind the bag! It gets through Buckner! Here comes Knight, and the Mets win it!" Scully paused for a few moments letting the pictures and the crowd noise tell the story. He resumed with, "If one picture is worth a thousand words, you have seen about a million words, but more than that, you have seen an absolutely bizarre finish to Game 6 of the 1986 World Series. The Mets are not only alive, they are well, and they will play the Red Sox in Game 7 tomorrow."

I tried to console my father by saying, "Hey, it's only Game 6, they'll come back tomorrow and take 'em down."

My optimism briefly brightened his spirits. I decided not to watch Game 7 with him due to our bad karma that year with Maine and the Red Sox. I believed mixing up our routine would help the Sox. It didn't, Boston blew a Game 7 lead and lost the series.

I called Ann and only half-kiddingly told her, "I'm so sorry; better keep him busy and close for a few days."

Chapter Eighteen
Southern Comfort

Three weeks after graduating from Boston College and three weeks before getting married, I started work at the Brown-Forman Corporation as a merchandising manager assigned to the North Shore region of Massachusetts. Brown-Forman makes, bottles, imports, exports, and markets whiskey, bourbon, tequila, and other alcohol under a variety of brand names, including Jack Daniel's, Southern Comfort, and Canadian Mist.

Yes, I took a job promoting alcohol. My job was to learn the business by building displays and gaining placements of Brown-Forman products in liquor stores. The company provided a van and hooked us up with a Realtor to find housing in Massachusetts. We rented an affordable apartment in the Montserrat neighborhood of Beverly, a small oceanside city just north of Boston. Martha was able to transfer within Carroll Reed, a women's clothing store chain that operated a shop in nearby Hamilton.

I don't think Martha was concerned about me working in the spirits industry. However, after my drunken wedding-night debacle I still harbored some doubts about my ability to handle alcohol. Frankly, it all centered on my family history. Emerging from that environment, I increasingly questioned and analyzed my actions, and understood I needed to remain vigilant about my alcohol use.

I often sounded like a young Walter when I would declare, "There's no way I have a drinking problem." But, did I? There is an old saying that you should keep your friends close and enemies closer; given that I was now working in the alcohol business, I was about to live with the enemy every day.

Once Martha and I returned from our honeymoon, we settled into our flat in Beverly. A week later I attended a ten-day national training meeting in Louisville. I was excited since I'd get to explore the hometown of one of my heroes, Muhammad Ali, and I would only be two hours from my aunt's house in Indianapolis and I could visit her. Of course, this was my first business trip, so most days the other trainees and I would be engrossed in role playing, case studies, and industry-related seminars. It was organized and professional. Each night after dinner was a mandatory cocktail party.

Two of these shindigs were unnerving.

The first event was a meet-and-greet with key company executives. Naturally, it featured an open bar. Since I didn't care much for hard liquor, I ordered a beer and mingled. A senior vice president strolled over to our group of trainees and pontificated on Brown-Forman. The man was in his early 60s and already half in the bag. He was personable enough, even charming in his inebriated state. At one point he eyeballed me and said, "Son, is that a beer in your hand? Let me inform you that we don't make beer at Brown-Forman."

I got the message. I gracefully removed myself, walked to the bar and ordered a Canadian Mist and ginger ale. What I really wanted to say was, "Why the fuck are you serving beer if I can't drink it." I thought better of that, but it was a test and I had failed. A few nights later that same man, after another company cocktail party, got into his car and crashed it into another vehicle.

On the same evening as the accident I was at a party with the training director and his team. Once again the event featured an open bar and everyone was getting shit-faced. At some point the training director called for our attention to make a toast. He lifted his glass and said, "Trainees, over seventy-five percent of the people in this business are divorced and over fifty percent are alcoholics, so drink up."

He knocked down his Early Times and water in one gulp. The toast and the scene were unsettling. I sipped my Canadian Mist and ginger ales all evening and might have been the only person in the room not wasted.

All I could think about was my father, and one nagging question:

"Should I be in this business?

I was suddenly in a place I never thought I would be—an oblivious dude drinking and promoting alcohol. My conscience was bothering me in a big way. Once again, my mother's voice was in my head: "If you drink you will be just like your father: drunk and living on the streets."

As soon as I got back to the hotel room I called Martha.

"Babe, sorry it's late, I just got back to the room and needed to call you."

"No problem. How was your day?"

"The training was good, but the evening was, how can I describe it? Disturbing."

"What happened?"

"Well, two nights ago an SVP gave me shit for drinking a beer at the cocktail party. He thought I should be drinking his products. He could barely stand up, and he's giving me grief about a beer. Anyway, about an hour ago the training director gave a toast, and this is what he spit out: Over seventy percent of the people in this business are divorced and over fifty percent are alcoholics. I was paralyzed for like a minute."

"Oh my god! Eddie, I'm so sorry."

"I know, unbelievable. I've been married less than a month; my father is an alcoholic, and these idiots are toasting divorce and alcoholism like it's no big deal. I wanted to puke. What the hell have I signed up for?"

The line was quiet for a moment.

"Don't worry. Give it time. We know what liquor does to people. Sounds like this director is a mess. Keep your head up; take it slow at the parties, and I'll be here when you get back."

"You better be."

I would actually stay at Brown-Forman for another two years, but that toast marked the beginning of the end. I knew I couldn't make working at the company a career. I just couldn't get over that night and would begin looking for a way out.

But first, before we knew what hit us, we moved to Texas. In January 1987, I got promoted and headed to Houston, the No. 1 liquor market in the country. In my new job, I worked in on-premise sales, meaning sales to restaurants and clubs. This new job had its perks as I was expected to frequent my customers regularly. That was great on the restaurant side because the food in Texas, from steak to Tex-Mex to Cajun, was outstanding. We dined out a lot. The downside was the clubs. They were fun, but I was out on the town many nights doing promotions and regularly drinking our product, primarily Canadian Mist or Southern Comfort. Also, five of my top ten accounts were strip joints, which were very popular. Naturally, Martha didn't have any interest in joining me at those promotions, and she wasn't thrilled that I had to "work" at them all the time. Given that nights featured lots of drinking and watching women dance while taking their clothes off, the training director in

Me with Red Auerbach, president of the Boston Celtics.

Louisville was spot on when he said the business was not conducive to a healthy marriage.

Rather than dwell on the negatives, Martha quickly found work at Laura Ashley, another textile design company, and set out to explore South Texas and Louisiana whenever possible. We grew to love Houston, but since my territory stretched from Bourbon Street in New Orleans to the River Walk in San Antonio we had a lot of ground to cover. We combined work and pleasure as much as possible. Perks included promotions on Sixth Street at the University of Texas in Austin, parties on South Padre Island, and Mardi Gras in Galveston. We also enjoyed Hurricanes on Bourbon Street and met Red Auerbach, president of the Boston Celtics, while sipping Southern Comfort Slam Dunks at the 1987 Final Four in New Orleans. The culinary highlight of our stay was an introduction to crawfish, jambalaya, and gumbo in the heart of Cajun country. Martha impressed the locals with her rendition of the

Cajun two-step while dining at Mulate's restaurant which showcased a dazzling dance floor. I also tried the two-step, but I suspect a few patrons are still recovering from having to watch my clumsy attempts.

Not surprisingly, family members scheduled vacations to visit us in Texas; after all, none of our parents or siblings had ever been. Sorry to say, Walter and Ann couldn't visit. I understood, since we couldn't afford to come home, either. It wasn't just lack of money; given that Walter was trying to stay sober, they opted not to travel much.

In July 1987, Martha's parents were the first to visit. Her father was a former minor league baseball player and he was excited that Brown-Forman had season tickets to the Houston Astros games. I reserved the tickets, which were situated right behind the third-base dugout. We were thrilled to visit NASA with them before settling into the Astrodome for the game. Late in the game, Astros outfielder Terry Puhl stepped into the batter's box and on the first pitch sliced a foul ball right at us. It bounced once and came right to Bud. He was ecstatic and had that ball mounted on his mantel back home for years. About a month later I also caught my first foul ball. Darryl Strawberry was in Houston with the New York Mets and he hit a towering pop-up into the row of seats directly behind us. I got lucky because the fan cupped his hands above his head trying to catch the ball and it bounced off him and right into my awaiting arms. It wasn't pretty, but I was thrilled. It was also kind of fitting, I felt the New York Mets owed me one.

Amazingly, Ma also got on a jet and came to visit us that fall. It was momentous since Ma had never been on a plane. She was afraid of heights. When I was 15 Ma, Walt, and I took the Greyhound Bus from Portland to visit Aunt Millie in Indianapolis. She said there was no way in hell she would ever get on a plane. We were shocked when Ma called and told us she was flying to Houston for a visit with her grandson, Bruce.

I asked her, "Why the change of heart about getting on a plane?"

"It's too far to go on the bus, and Bruce is flying with me. Gin is picking up the fare, and suggested some good pills to get me through the flight."

I laughed and told her, "OK, no turning back now. We'll see you at the airport in a few weeks."

Ma was always a history buff. She was excited to walk the grounds of the Alamo and visit NASA. The flight arrived on schedule and it was funny watching my mother and my 12-year-old nephew disembark the plane. Although she denied it, she appeared a bit tipsy. Whatever drugs she took to get her through the flight were still working. My nephew was exhausted. Basically, he babysat and held his grandmother's hand for the entire trip. He was delighted to see us, if for no other reason than to take a break from his grandmother. Ma was her classic self. Houston is seventy-five miles wide and the airport sits in the northeast corner. Our apartment was in the southwest corner of the city, so it took a while to get home. Regrettably for us, the drugs wore off and she complained the entire ride back to our place.

A few days later we took them to San Antonio. Bruce was eager to visit Sea World while Ma was anxious to see the Alamo. For dinner we stuffed ourselves with enchiladas and burritos while watching the barges pass by the banks of the River Walk. The rides to and fro were unforgettable, filled with ageless Ma witticisms. Ma always needed to sit in the shotgun seat. And being a nervous Nellie, she never shut up. It's a four-hour drive each way from Houston to San Antonio, so Martha was perfectly fine sitting in the back with Bruce since it provided what little peace and quiet one could find in our sedan. The trip got off to a rocky start when about an hour west of Houston on I-10 we got pulled over by a Texas state trooper. When I saw the lights flash I immediately glanced at the speedometer and noted we were going approximately sixty-two miles per hour. The speed limit at the time was fifty-five. Since cars were passing me just before getting pulled over I assumed something else was wrong, maybe a light was out or the inspection was overdue. Ma was immediately in a tizzy since she wanted to be in San Antonio as soon as the gates opened at the Alamo. When the trooper approached the driver's side window, I handed him my license and registration and asked him why he pulled us over.

"I clocked you going sixty-two in the fifty-five zone."

I thought that was lame, but I shrugged it off expecting only a warning. Well, the young trooper came back, ticket in hand, and wished us a good day. Ma wasn't having any of that. She looked at the trooper and yelled at him.

"You pulled us over because we are from Maine!"

I did all I could not to laugh. I knew my license, registration, and plates were all from Texas. This poor trooper had no idea he was dealing with Maniacs. I tried to explain this to Ma, but she was convinced and would not let it go. It was so Ma, so provincial, all we could do was shake our heads and acquiesce to her logic.

The ride home was more bizarre. Somehow our conversation turned to kids and sex. Ma seemed oblivious that there was a 12-year old sitting in the back seat. At one point, she blurted out, "I only had sex eight times and it was always in the dark."

I looked in the rear-view mirror. Martha was aghast and Bruce was on the edge of his seat. She went on to explain that she didn't like sex very much, but that it was the Christian thing to do. Martha and I could barely contain ourselves. Bruce was both enthralled and embarrassed.

I jokingly suggested, "Ma, I think we should head to Las Vegas because with your perfect record when having sex (eight times, eight children) we could clean out the casinos and retire for good."

She got the message and changed the topic, much to Bruce's chagrin.

Overall, aside from some backward attitudes in the 1980s (some folks always eyed me suspiciously as a "Yankee") and occasionally some not-so-subtle racism (the N-word was thrown around with ease by some folks), we fell in love with Houston. We met and made some wonderful friends, but it just wasn't the right time in our lives to stay for very long in the state, or in the liquor business. We were thinking about babies and moving closer to home.

As we rolled into 1988, I focused on finding another job and soon Martha and I packed our bags and moved to New Jersey where I would work as a regional sales manager in the picture-framing industry at Nielsen & Bainbridge. My new territory included New York City, New Jersey, and eastern Pennsylvania. Martha was able to transfer within Laura Ashley, and we were psyched to be back within driving distance of Maine.

Our first child, Seth, was born on July 27 in Hackensack, New Jersey. Seth was the fifth grandchild and the fourth grandson for Walter, who seemed to really love being Grampy, which was remarkable and heartwarming since he'd blown being a dad. Walt's son, Tim, and Carolyn's three children, Keagan, Karinna, and Mikail, all lived in Maine and were building wonderful relationships with Walter.

Meanwhile, my relationship with him, and by extension that of my children, continued to develop in fits and starts. During my four years away, I kept in touch with my father sporadically. Unlike today when staying connected through social media is easy, in the 1980s and early 1990s, staying connected meant writing a letter or calling on the telephone. Neither Walter nor I were very good at that. As a result, whatever momentum toward true reconciliation that we'd gained working together at his painting business back in 1985 stalled out when we did not live in the same area code. In addition, from a financial standpoint, times remained tough for Walter and Ann, so traveling to New Jersey was no better an option than flying to Texas.

When we moved to New Jersey we planned to visit Maine more frequently, but life has a funny way of changing the best laid plans. Our jobs were demanding, including frequent weekend work, so getting home often just wasn't in the cards. Moreover, just two months after moving to New Jersey, we learned Martha was pregnant, further limiting our travel plans and grounding us even more. It wasn't until Thanksgiving that my father met Seth. Walter sang him a lullaby.

Like Houston, we thoroughly enjoyed living just outside New York City. Hawthorne, New Jersey, is only twenty minutes from Midtown Manhattan. The majority of my customers were in the five boroughs, so I spent hours upon hours on the streets and highways in and around the Big Apple. Thankfully, my time there coincided with the rise of the legendary Mike and the Mad Dog sports talk radio show on WFAN. Their fun banter and endless arguing over everything, including plenty of smack talk about Boston sports, kept me entertained as I sat stuck in traffic. Due to Martha's pregnancy we didn't get to explore the area as much as we did in Texas and Louisiana. Still, we took in our first Broadway show and spent New Year's Eve in Times Square watching the ball drop. Martha was also trying to add a little culture to my life.

One afternoon while pitching picture frame equipment in Midtown I even stumbled upon Trump Tower. The building was massive, a true skyscraper, and just a few blocks down Fifth Avenue from the renowned toy store FAO Schwarz, our favorite shop in the city.

As a curious tourist, I waltzed right into Trump Tower and thought, "There must be a lookout at the top of this building." I got on the elevator and hit the button for the top floor. Boy, was I in for a surprise. By the time the elevator reached the top, I was the only person left in the box. I thought nothing of this development. When the doors opened I stepped out straight into a large lobby, and immediately began to have second thoughts. I glanced to my right and standing not ten feet away was the future President of the United States, Donald J. Trump. I vaguely recall Trump nodding his head as two very big and intimidating men began to approach me. Instinctively, I smiled at the two guys and said, "Sorry, wrong floor," and stepped right back into the elevator.

Although we were happy in New Jersey, Seth's birth had us aching for home, or at least for being a little closer to Portland. I kept my eyes open for a new job. When I learned that a commercial bakery, Lepage Bakeries in Auburn, was looking for a marketing executive to build their business in and beyond the state, I jumped at it. I got the job and we celebrated Seth's first birthday in Maine, while waiting for our new home to be built in a field where Martha played as a child. We could not have been more blessed.

Walter and Ann's house in Scarborough was less than a half-hour away from our new place. I never expected to use the words career and my father in the same sentence, but he was now leading the custodial staff at a local school district and loving it. Ann had hung out her own counseling shingle and was practicing the craft with her usual vigor.

Shortly after moving into our home in November and hosting family holiday festivities, we had more wonderful news to share. Martha was pregnant again. Our beautiful daughter Mattie would arrive in October 1991. Walter and I got very busy that summer. Since he still had all the equipment, he insisted on helping me paint our house. Our days were similar to when we worked together painting in 1985, but with a twist—this was a labor of love. Nobody was getting paid. Of course, I couldn't render my usual barter for such services, which was a case of beer or liquor of choice. Instead, we enjoyed each other's company. Still, I couldn't shake the memories of those lost years. I couldn't get past the feeling that if I got close to my father, I was somehow betraying my mother or condoning his past behavior. Somewhere in the back of my mind, I was still the teenager who sprinted from his drunken father as he wandered into a group of friends begging for money without recognition. Or the kid overcome by anxiety every time he walked through Lincoln Park, hoping to not see his father passed out on a bench.

I just wouldn't let my father get too close. I'm sure he sensed it, but he never said a word. My loyalty was *always* to my mother and it was clear. I'm convinced this made him more tentative around my family, because he didn't take the initiative to be involved with our children when they were young. I was disappointed that he didn't embrace a more grandfatherly role with my children. Especially since he did with his other grandchildren, and some of them lived hours away.

Martha and I would discuss it, and I'd try to take the blame for any disconnect. However, I really wasn't sure why, and I was uncomfortable addressing it. Although this unspoken dynamic bubbled just below the surface for years, I was convinced that our relationship was just fine. Maybe my expectations were unrealistic, maybe he wasn't comfortable, or more likely he was waiting for *me* to be more inviting and fully embrace him despite my lingering unease and caution.

Whatever the reality, despite flickering moments of change, my father, even now that he was a grandfather, peered from the shadows while my mother stayed front and center in the light—just like always.

This is my daughter Mattie and me, around 1996.

Chapter Nineteen
The Ice Storm

Every year, I sent my mother a Father's Day card.

She was the most inspirational person in my life. She was dealt a bad hand and she served the role of both mother and father while Walter begged for money or was passed out on the streets. The card was my way of telling her I recognize the sacrifices she made for me; that I knew she abandoned whatever dreams she had for the good of her children.

I am a big believer in role models. I believe family, friends, coaches, and teachers have much more impact on your life than any athlete on the diamond or star on the silver screen, no matter how high on a pedestal society places them or how hard we root for or idolize them. I always looked close to home for role models and I tried to adopt the good traits of those who played a role in my life, while discarding the bad, in hopes of becoming a better person.

That instinct wasn't just a platitude that sounded good, I actually did it. Like many folks, I also seemed to recall more easily and hold close the slights or gestures of disrespect, real or imagined, that came my way over the years more so than I did the graciousness bestowed on me by so many. For some reason, when someone lets you down, disappoints you, or flat out betrays you, it burns hotter and stays with you much longer.

That was certainly the case with my father. I thought I was doing the right thing, but it wasn't until the twenty-first century, nearly twenty years into his hard-fought sobriety, that I acknowledged my new relationship with my father was a house of cards, more show than substance. Both of us went through the motions, acting like all was fine and forgiven. It was just superficial. Truth be told, even when he was sober I still thought of my father as an anti-role model. Deep down I still saw him as that shitty father in the Harry Chapin song I had told him about years earlier in Orono. I didn't appreciate his struggle or what he had accomplished even as he was almost miraculously modifying his personal narrative. But soon even the shiny, fake veneer fell off of our relationship. What shook me even more was the role that Ann was playing in our strained relationship. She made it worse. Clearly Ann was protective of Walter and I did not see that coming. Due to her perception that I was not treating my father well, Ann developed an aversion toward me.

After we moved back to Maine, Martha and I added two beautiful children to our family tree, Martha Mary (Mattie) in 1991 and Edward Hannigan (Teddy) in 1997. From my perspective, throughout the 1990s, their paternal grandparents made little to no effort to see their grandchildren. In response I stubbornly mirrored their air of detachment.

Ann felt it was *my* responsibility to welcome Walter unconditionally. Since that wasn't happening, they withdrew even more. It was awkward; as the decade dragged on we'd go months without talking, always acting as if everything was good.

Bottom line: I had not forgiven my father. I couldn't get past what he did to me, to the family, and to Ma. I wasn't fully extending myself, and he chose not to push the issue. I was OK with that and I think to some degree he understood, but not Ann.

It would only get worse.

In January 1998, Greater Portland was hit with an ice storm for the ages. I was ten months into a new job with Parker-Tilton, a food broker in Scarborough located only three miles from my father's house. Occasionally, I would go to Amato's, pick up Italian sandwiches, and we'd eat lunch together at his house. Much of the area lost power for three to four days, while some towns remained without electricity for weeks. It was a trying and difficult time for nearly everyone. Walter and Ann were fortunate, they only lost heat for a day or two. It was January in Maine and we were at home in Portland freezing our asses off with no sign of improvement anytime soon. Officials and the media were telling folks to find shelter, to not wait out the storm in a cold home. It was dangerous. Unfortunately, we did not have a generator or a fireplace to keep our house cozy. I talked to my father almost daily giving him updates on our situation. Walter and Ann were the only local family members who had power, so we assumed our best option for shelter was their house. There we were with three young children, ages 9, 7, and 10 months, cowering for cover and huddling for heat, and there was no offer of refuge coming from the grandparents.

Martha grew increasingly incensed.

"Eddie, what is the deal? They're warm and cozy, while their grandkids are freezing. They know what's going on, and that we're looking for a place to stay, right?"

"Yes. We are going over for dinner tonight. I'm hoping they'll step up and offer to let us stay."

We arrived for dinner and Ann was distant. I laid it on thick, detailing our plight and limited options.

As the evening wore on the atmosphere in the room grew more and more uncomfortable. My father remained eerily quiet, which was discouraging.

At one point, he said: "It doesn't look like the power is coming back anytime soon. (The local weatherman Joe) Cupo is forecasting more sleet tonight. The power company can't keep up. Are you going back home tonight?"

"If it was just Martha and I, we'd probably stick it out at home. But with the kids, that seems ill-advised. All generators within a hundred miles are gone. We need someplace warm for them."

Then Ann *really* pissed us off.

"Getting a hotel room is a great idea," she said.

I had already checked the area hotels. There were no rooms available.

We chatted for a while longer before Martha, angry and impatient, moved to bring the night to a close.

"Hey, thanks for dinner. We should probably get going."

"OK, let's get the kids in their PJs before hitting the road," I said.

Finally, my father stepped up.

"Where are you going? Guys, this is crazy. You should stay here until the power is back at your house."

We were irritated, but had no choice. We accepted the offer and prepared the kids for their first warm night of sleep in nearly a week.

Ann was not pleased. I am sure Walter suffered her wrath after we left.

To this point, the strained relationship had remained exclusively the domain of us two men. The Ice Storm changed everything. Now, the two women were also at odds. Martha took Ann's comments as cruel and both of us felt that Ann seemed much too comfortable trying to cast us back into the bitter cold night, which elevated her to the top of our shit list. Martha is the nicest person

I've ever known, but be warned, slight her cubs and she can hold a grudge with the best of them.

Our relationship with Ann never recovered.

As for Walter, he and I would continue to eat lunch once in a while, but there weren't any full family gatherings, outside of holidays.

Chapter Twenty
The Music Men

The year 2001 was a personal odyssey, probably the most poignant year of my life. I was working at a start-up, a dot-com company in Portland, when it went belly up in June. I was almost 40 and suddenly unemployed for the first time in my adult life. With three kids, ages 4 to 12, and Martha working as a stay-at-home mom, life got complicated in a hurry. I immediately began networking, but struggled to gain any real traction. As a result, Martha jumped back into action, and prepared to start working as a substitute teacher that fall. By this time, Teddy was in all-day kindergarten and Martha's income would keep us from totally depleting our savings.

As summer wore on, some good job prospects and opportunities presented themselves and I entered into serious talks with two different companies and it all seemed very promising. That all came to halt on September 11. I was at home and *The Today Show* was playing in the background. From across the room, I heard a report that a plane had crashed into one of the World Trade Center towers. I dropped whatever I was doing and focused on the news. Moments later, Martha and I watched in horror as a second plane flew into the other tower.

My dad with Seth, his grandson in the late '90s.

One plane might have been an accident, but when the second hit, I knew we were under attack. We were scared. All I wanted to do was lock my doors, squeeze my babies, and pray for our lost heroes, their families, and friends. My unemployment became secondary, even unimportant, as tragedy, fear, and uncertainty gripped the nation. Of course, I wasn't surprised when the two companies immediately put all talks on hold. In the aftermath of the attacks, I didn't even get another informational interview for months.

Back in the spring, my old roommate, Mike, and I decided that running a marathon would be a good "turning 40 thing to do." We dreamed big and made plans to run the New York City Marathon. When we made the plan, I wasn't in any shape to run such a grueling race. I began training in earnest once we got the word around Memorial Day weekend that we won the lottery and were selected as participants in the race. Although losing my job a month later was bad news, the silver lining was it gave me time to get in shape.

I had plenty of time to travel to Lewiston and run with my good friend. I was losing weight and was excited to again soak in the sights and sounds of New York City on race day, the first Sunday in November. By Labor Day, I felt great. After 9/11, there was talk of canceling the marathon out of respect for those who perished in the attack, but marathon organizers and the city rallied, and the race went off as scheduled.

Unfortunately I didn't. The family was hit by a more personal tragedy—my nephew, Mikail Robert Russo, died unexpectedly on October 28, 2001. He was only 16.

Mikail was the third child of my sister Carolyn and her husband, Paul. Like Martha and me, and my parents, Carolyn and Paul had three children: a boy, a girl, and then another boy. Although she was only a year older than me, Carolyn started earlier when it came to children. Mikail was born in 1985, four years before Seth.

Mikail was the cousin closest in age to my kids, and he was a doting role model to them. He taught Seth and Mattie the right way to play Wiffle ball, kick a soccer ball, and shoot hoops. He even tried to help my golf game, an impossible task.

My father and Mikail were very close. It was no secret, Mikail was my father's favorite grandchild and they enjoyed a special kinship.

My brother David called to tell me what happened. I was in shock and remained so for days. The wake and funeral were performed with sensitivity and respect, but they were heartbreaking. The first person I saw when I walked into the wake was my father. He was a mess. He couldn't even speak. He was so despondent, I was truly concerned that he would resort to drinking again to ease his pain. I spent a lot of time with him over the next few days. We ate breakfast and lunch together each day and walked the streets of

Camden just talking. Everyone else was also on high alert regarding Walter. Mikail, his "little buddy," was gone.

As I said earlier, following the 1998 ice storm I became even more aloof toward Walter and Ann. I was angry and disappointed with them and made less of an effort to connect. As expected Walter did not push the issue and Ann didn't help at all, so other than holidays we rarely spoke.

To be honest, the iciness didn't really bother me. The huge wall I built between us wasn't easily penetrated. That said, I also began to realize that I wasn't being fair to my children who, because of all this, didn't really know their grandfather.

After Mikail's death, I decided to initiate outings with Walter and Ann. I felt it was the right thing to do. I took a deep breath. It was time for somebody to be the bigger person. It was time to forge ahead. Walter never had a relationship with me and now he didn't have one with my children. Prompted by Mikail's passing, I decided something needed to change.

Perhaps ironically, the Boston Red Sox, the team that caused my father so much pain over the years, played a key role in helping us to begin to make that change.

In January 2002, after six months of unemployment, I found a job. I started at Hannaford, a regional grocery store chain with headquarters in Maine. The job was a lifesaver. I received the offer on Christmas Eve, so the good news meant 2001, a miserable year, ended on a high note. As a bonus, working at Hannaford meant we would stay in Maine, which made Martha and the kids happy.

One perk of working for Hannaford was that it gave me access to tickets to sporting events. In May, I got four tickets to an August game at Fenway Park between the Red Sox and the Yankees. Martha suggested I ask my father. I had been thinking about asking him, but planned to ask her and our two oldest children first. Martha gracefully bowed out, and my father could not have been more excited. My father was always a massive Red Sox fan. His most prized possession during his years on the streets was a Red Sox cap and he was rarely seen without one as he wandered the streets of Portland. He had watched on television and listened on the radio to thousands of games, but he had never been to Fenway Park.

"This is a dream come true," he told me.

On game day, Walter came to the house early to watch Seth play in a Babe Ruth league game. After Seth's game, Seth tossed his grandfather my baseball glove so they could have a game of catch.

About five minutes in, Seth urged my father on.

"Come on, Grampy, you can throw it harder than that. Bring it!"

"I'm not young like you anymore. This arm is a bit stiff."

"You sound like Dad. He says the same thing."

Seth's comments brought a smile to my father's face. I know, because I watched it all unfold from behind a curtain in our living room. I struggled to hold back the tears.

"Eddie, what's wrong?" Martha asked.

"Nothing, absolutely nothing," I whimpered.

"Check it out," I said pointing to Seth and my father. "I've never, ever played catch with my father."

She gave me a peck on the cheek.

"Why don't you go join them?"

"I'm good. I don't think I could hold it together."

Our Fenway seats were in the .406 Club, a section named after Ted Williams, the last major leaguer to hit over .400. The .406 Club was right behind home plate, and our seats were in the front row. I still get giddy thinking about it. We got to our seats, gloves in hand, two hours early to watch batting practice. Walter never sat down. He stared at the field, his field of dreams, and commented on every intricacy of the ballpark, from the Eire-like grass to the Green Monster to the Pesky Pole.

"Dad, would you like a Fenway Frank?" I asked.

"Definitely, but not right yet. I can't believe how green the field is. It's like pictures of Ireland. It's really kind of blinding … And it's manicured so beautifully."

"Damn it, I didn't bring a camera," I said.

"That's alright, don't need one. I've already taken a picture with my eyes. I'll never forget it."

Although the .406 Club was enclosed in plexiglass, my father sat in his seat with my baseball glove on his hand. The only time he took it off was to savor his Fenway Frank.

In addition to baseball, my father's other passion was music. As it turns out, not long after our trip to Fenway, Seth played Winthrop in a middle school production of *The Music Man*. To my surprise, Walter knew both the play and the character. Despite Martha's attempt at adding some culture to my life, I hadn't heard of either of them. Lyman Moore Middle School had an outstanding theater program, but I didn't know my son was interested. I was taken aback when he came home and told us that he'd auditioned for the play.

When Seth informed us that he got the part of Winthrop, he was rather flippant about it. I asked if he wanted to rent the movie and he said, "No thanks," so I left it alone. *The Music Man* is set in small Midwestern town where a con artist poses as a bandleader to sell instruments and uniforms, planning to skip town after he collected all the residents' cash. The town librarian sees through the con man, but she falls in love with him after he helps her younger brother, Winthrop, overcome a lisp and social awkwardness.

I arrived early on opening night with Martha, Mattie, and Teddy. Surprisingly, my father and Ann were sitting in the second row. They were the first to arrive. The play was a smash and all the kids were fabulous. In my humble opinion, Seth stole the show. The Winthrop role, if done properly, requires a convincing speech impediment. Seth nailed it because he spoke all his lines and sang all his songs with a lisp. In spite of that, his singing was strong, and his performance had everybody buzzing.

At the end of the play, I sat there with this huge smile.

Looking at my father, I said, "Oh my God, where did that come from?"

Seth always loved music, but I had no idea he had great pipes and acting chops. My father, who dreamed of being a singer, leaned over to me with tears rolling down his cheeks.

"That's what I always wanted to do."

I gave him a hug. And for the first time ever, I looked at my father and said: "I love you."

In the wake of the Red Sox game and Seth's performance, we saw quite a bit of my father for the next eight years, thanks primarily to his grandchildren's performances. My children were finally forming a connection with their grandfather. Martha and I stressed balance to our children. Rather than focus on one sport or activity exclusively, we encouraged them to try them all. This philosophy kept us, and them, very busy year round. By high school, Seth was running cross-country in the fall, shooting hoops in the winter, and slicing tennis balls in the spring. Mattie went the field hockey, basketball, softball route, while Teddy ran cross-country and played ice hockey and lacrosse. I would forward all their schedules to Walter. Although he rarely showed up at sporting events, he never missed a play.

Seth followed up his middle school performance in *The Music Man* with a supporting role in *Guys and Dolls* and the lead in *Schoolhouse Rock*. During his sophomore year at Portland High School, my alma mater, Seth won the lead role of Sky Masterson in *Guys and Dolls*. The high school plays were much longer than the middle school versions and much more demanding. Walter could not wait to watch Seth perform. He related to the New York City set and the hustle that was the way of his youth. Throw in the play's inherent religious overtones and it was a trip down memory lane.

Seth's performance as Sky Masterson didn't bring tears to Walter's eyes, just a broad, beaming smile. His presentation took Walter back in time to memories of playing dice on the streets. At times in his youth Walter thought of himself as Sky Masterson, and now had lived long enough to see his grandson play the part. Following the scene when Seth nailed the song, "Luck Be a Lady," Walter leaned over to Ann and said, "That was me. And Jeep. In the Bowery."

My heart skipped a beat.

As fate would have it, Walter got a do-over on this scene when Teddy was cast as Sky Masterson five years later. This time the tears flowed.

My sons fueled my dad's passion for music. It was quite common for a sing-along to break out when Walter visited. He had a distinguished deep voice and wasn't shy about belting out tunes. Understandably, Seth, and even Teddy who was now actively participating in these impromptu concerts, were not familiar with any of Walter's favorites, but these really were delightful sessions.

After graduating from Portland High, Seth was accepted into the prestigious S.I. Newhouse School of Public Communications at Syracuse University. Seth, like his grandfather, possessed a strong, deep voice and he entertained thoughts of being a broadcaster. He had dabbled in broadcasting in high school, calling play-by-play at some basketball games. An admissions official from another school declared during our college tour, "The Newhouse School is the Harvard of communication schools." Seth was pumped to be an Orangeman and in Newhouse.

At Syracuse he saw a poster seeking interested parties to audition for a production of *Urinetown*. Again, as in middle school, Seth didn't tell anyone he was going to audition. Like then, he got a part in the play. We went to the production, and it was fabulous. The sets, costumes, and voices were incredible. Walter couldn't make the trip to Syracuse, but he found solace in the storyline. The basic plot of *Urinetown* is that because of a water shortage private facilities have become undrinkable. To control water consumption, people have to pay to use the public toilets for their "private business." Walter thought this was hilarious—he spent half his life sneaking into public restrooms to do his business.

While at home for winter break, Seth seemed to spend an exorbitant amount of time in his room listening to the hit song "Empire State of Mind" by Jay-Z and Alicia Keys. Finally, curiosity got the best of me, and I invaded the sacred space of a teenager's room to ask, "What's with playing that song over and over and over again?"

He laughed, "I'm writing a parody. Calling it "Portland State of Mind."

He handed me a draft of his song. It blew me away! The family feedback was positive, so Seth submitted it to a local radio station, WJBQ. Not only did WJBQ play the song, but they invited Seth into the studio to talk about it. When Walter heard the song, his jaw dropped. He knew Portland better than most and thought Seth captured the essence of his city perfectly.

Seth had rekindled his grandfather's passion. For them, music never skipped a beat.

Chapter Twenty-One
A Standing Ovation

M y mother wanted to see all of her grandchildren's
performances, athletic or otherwise. She was ten years older
than Walter and as she entered her 80s, her health was in decline.
Martha or I would pick her up and bring her to as many events as
possible. She preferred sports activities to the theater shows. She
loved sports, whether it was watching games or talking about them.
She went to every race, game, or match on the schedule, as long as
we picked her up (she never did get her driver's license). One of my
huge regrets is not taking her to *every* event.

Ma died on March 4, 2009. She was 86.

Even in her final days, she was sharp as a tack. Her passing was
unexpected and sudden. After my grandmother died in December
of 1986, 60 Kellogg Street was given to my brother Jimmy. When it
sold a few years later, Ma moved first to Franklin Towers and then
to Park Danforth in the late-1990s. On Friday, February 27, Teddy
and I dropped by Ma's apartment at Park Danforth to watch our
beloved Boston Celtics. The Celtics were playing the Indiana Pacers which meant Ma was somewhat calm since "Larry Legend,"
Larry Bird, was working for the Pacers. If there wasn't some Celtics
connection on the opposing team, she hated that team. Her spirits were high, and she was feeling good. The Green beat the Pacers

and all was well in the world. Teddy had no interest in the game, so she talked his ear off while I watched the game. When we left that night I had no inkling she'd be gone within the week.

I made plans to stop by on Sunday to visit Ma and run some errands. Before arriving, I received a call from Carolyn, who was at Ma's place. "Ma's spitting up blood. We need to get her to the hospital," she said. Carolyn summoned an ambulance to transport Ma to Maine Medical Center. We called our siblings to tell them what was going on. Ma looked fine, except for a disgusting tar-like substance coming from her lungs. The nurses moved Ma into a holding room and administered multiple tests. They tried to keep her calm, but that was difficult since her eyes were glued to the TV. The Celtics were playing the hated Detroit Pistons, and Ma didn't want to be bothered with questions. Now these weren't the despised Detroit "Bad Boys" from 1990s fame, but she still associated these Pistons teams with their predecessors. She recalled Johnny Most screaming at McNasty, Bill Laimbeer, and McFilthy, Rick Mahorn, and her venom came rushing back. The doctors didn't get much out of her until the game was over.

Tests showed Ma had pneumonia. I couldn't believe how quickly it developed. Here it was Sunday afternoon and the doctors were telling me that this pneumonia had my mother in dire shape. I thought, "Wait a minute, everything was fine thirty-six hours ago, and now you're telling me she's not responding to medication, and it's touch and go?" I was upset and confused. From Sunday to Tuesday, Ma went downhill fast. They put a tube in her on Monday to help her breathe, and it killed her spirit. It was apparent that she did not have the strength to fight pneumonia, but she battled. Finally, late Tuesday evening the doctors informed us that the only things keeping Ma alive were the machines. Her eight children faced the most emotional and difficult decision of their lives.

After midnight all of Ma's children and their spouses gathered in a conference room. Earlier the doctors had explained Ma's situation. She had been given several heart medications and she was on a respirator to keep her breathing. We were told that the heart medicine was ineffective and without the respirator she could not breathe on her own.

Lengthy and agonizing discussion followed. My brother-in-law Bruce and sister-in-law Anna shared their experiences of the difficulty deciding when to let a parent go. Also, a couple questions arose about Ma's medications, the respirator, and her prognosis.

Jimmy met with doctors, and they reviewed our options. Basically the doctors gave us two choices. We could keep her on the respirator and pray that she got better. However, it was clear the doctors did not support that choice. In fact, one of them said, "The chance of her coming back is slim to none." Our second choice, and the one supported by the doctors, was to remove the tubes and prepare for the inevitable, but hope for a miracle.

I didn't want to watch my mother gasping for her last breath and trying to fight off certain death. Rather than go into the hospital room and wait for my mother to die, I paced the corridors of Maine Medical Center.

Not surprisingly, Ma put up a fight. What was expected to last twenty seconds, turned into nearly twenty minutes. Thanks to the drugs it wasn't so much a struggle, but more a slow drift to sleep. That made me happy. The memory of Ma laughing it up with Teddy days earlier stays lodged as my final memory.

We all knew Ma wanted a wake and funeral; after all, that was the Catholic tradition. My oldest brother David took charge and made arrangements to meet with the funeral home director that afternoon. He asked me to join him. He wrote the obituary, but he wanted me to proof it so that nothing was missed. It needed to be as politically correct as possible considering our modern family. Other than a few quick fixes, David's obituary, as expected, was perfect. We scheduled Ma's wake for Friday evening, and her funeral for Saturday morning.

At my mother's wake I overheard a friend of hers call us "The Miracle Family." That was the ultimate compliment to my Mom. To some, my family seemed special because we beat the odds and the stereotypes. Even so "The Miracle Family" comment surprised me and in all sincerity I asked the lady, "What do you mean?"

She said, "All eight of you made a good life; you came out the other side. Your mother was very proud."

She was right, Ma batted one thousand. All eight of her children matured to be good citizens and constructive contributors to their communities, despite the odds and some people's prediction the cycle of poverty and alcoholism would continue as it did for so many on Munjoy Hill. Yes, we'd find our way into alcohol and drugs, spend some time in jail, and regrettably lose one or two along the way. How did we emerge comparatively unscathed when so many others didn't? Was it dumb luck? No, we had a miracle worker, my Mom, our rock.

While meeting with the funeral home director I began thinking about how to properly honor my mother. I spent the next couple of days going through pictures for a slideshow at the wake, and more importantly pondering how to eulogize Ma. I'm not sure if my siblings expected me to write something, it was never discussed, but I took it upon myself to offer and nobody objected. I was comfortable writing the eulogy, but I wasn't sure if I could get through it. I talked to Danny about what to say, and he was immensely helpful. We both questioned whether we could hold it together and determined that was unlikely. Although Danny was still willing to try, I looked at him and suggested, "Let's have Seth do it?"

He grinned and said, "Perfect."

We called Seth over and gave him the news. He hadn't even seen the words, but he smiled and said, "I'd be honored."

Seth delivered the following eulogy at my mother's funeral:

"This is for Gram, or as all her kids know her, Ma.

"Some people are simply better than the rest of us, and hopefully at times, we who love them, tell them. Gram, you were so beautiful, so strong, so resilient and so patient. You defined the word family. Somehow over the years you managed to take care of your eight kids and their spouses, their children, and their children's children. You remembered everyone, every birthday, every holiday, every graduation, first communion, anniversary ... We even received cards for Easter, St. Patrick's Day, and Valentine's. But here's the truly amazing thing ... you had so little yourself, but loved giving to family more than anything else.

"My Uncle Danny recalls taking a little cart with his Mom to get the free surplus food for folks on welfare. He was embarrassed walking back up Munjoy Hill because people saw him, and knew. Later when in college it struck him how Ma must have felt. But Ma, a bright, capable, beautiful person didn't care what anyone thought; she did what she needed to do for her family.

"My dad, and her son, Eddie, shared another story this week. He had come home from college and helped Ma do her taxes. He was shocked to realize that Ma's annual income never exceeded $3,000 a year. Welfare and food stamps were her lifelines. How did she keep it all together? Now we know—she was actually the richest lady around. Her riches were loving, caring and giving. She understood what family meant, and through her selflessness, epitomized family at its best.

"Uncle Danny shared a recent conversation he had with Ma— she asked what his son needed for Christmas, and he responded by saying he didn't need anything and told her to keep the money for herself. Then he thought, 'How silly of me,' and at once appreciated that this was her way, always trying to give.

"Ma loved sports and never stopped sharing it with all of us. She bled Celtic green, which explains why while in the emergency room last Sunday, she would not look away from her beloved Celtics, and her latest favorite player, No. 20 Ray Allen, to listen to the doctor ask about her meds. To her, loyalty was instinctive and essential. We all knew she expected that, especially from family—her home team. She was a homer and we were blessed to have this amazing supporter. *Always.* Ma was so capable of individual achievement, yet for whatever reasons always chose family first, before her own personal growth. Amazingly for the times, she never drove a car or cared about much that benefited her directly. Early on she established her priorities and fortunately for us we were the priority.

"Upon hearing the sad news of her passing, a friend who knew the family well said, 'Right now she and her mom are sharing a cup of tea, keeping an eye on all of you.' That was Ma.

"Another family friend posted this note on the Conroy-Tully website: 'An amazing story of sacrifice, devotion and love began on February 17, 1923. It's the story of Virginia Crockett that her eight children Marie, Virginia, Carolyn, David, Jimmy, Danny, Walter, and Eddie, all knew well, since they lived it. Munjoy Hill (God's Country in Portland, Maine) provided the backdrop for this legend. Your mother's story is widely known to community people like me and is one to cherish, laugh about, cry about, and most certainly to tell and retell over the years to follow.'

"Grammy, we all miss you and love you. In closing, I want to give you, the ultimate giver, a warm and resounding 'Thank you.'"

After he finished the eulogy, Seth moved to the side of the pulpit and started clapping. The entire congregation rose to their feet and gave Ma a standing ovation.

Writing my mother's eulogy was energizing. She was a simple gal with a big heart. She was a giver, and I wanted to give her something back. I figured my mother, the greatest champion of her children, her family, her friends, and all New England sports teams, deserved to be recognized in a special way.

I contemplated, "How about a standing ovation for a job well done?"

After much deliberation I determined that concluding Ma's eulogy with a standing ovation was the proper tribute. After the funeral Seth acknowledged that he had never been more nervous in his life. You would not have known it. He was flawless. His move to the left of the podium, with just the right amount of pause, to start the standing ovation for Ma was magical. The congregation was on its feet before I could even lift out of my chair, and I knew it was coming.

Many in attendance commented, "I've never seen anything like that at a funeral. That was cool."

Well, they'd never seen anyone, ever, like my mother. She earned it.

Chapter Twenty-Two
Saving Lives

For years, Walter Crockett thought Alcoholics Anonymous was pure bullshit.

As a young man in his 20s and early 30s, Walter was cocky and arrogant. He'd tell his wife, his friends, his siblings, and anyone who would listen that he could stop drinking any time he wanted. He was convinced that he was in control. He was delusional. Shortly after returning home from the Army, Walter occasionally went to AA meetings at the request of my Uncle Brud. However, he didn't take them seriously and only went to get Brud off his back. Uncle Brud was a recovering alcoholic, and knew an alcoholic when he saw one. He knew Walter was in trouble, but couldn't get through to his brother. Uncle Brud hoped marrying Ginny, a teetotaler, would give his little brother the necessary support and a reason to stay clean. In all likelihood, marriage and fatherhood had the opposite effect; Walter drank to escape his responsibility. He simply crumbled under the pressure.

Just a few months before Ginny kicked Walter out for good, Brud had told her, "We can't help him if he won't help himself."

It took seventeen years of denial, living on the streets, and five brushes with death before Walter took responsibility and began to accept that he was an alcoholic. Eventually, he also began to trust AA and that helped pave his path to sobriety.

Even in sobriety, Walter suffered bouts of depression and fought urges to drink, but as far as anyone knew he never imbibed again. As he walked his personal mental tightrope, his sanctuary was AA. In the aftermath of his release from Togus, Walter attended AA meetings every day, sometimes more than once. When he was not working, he drove all over southern Maine to participate in AA discussions. He built each day around his work schedule and an AA gathering. Every night when he came home, Ann left a cold Diet Pepsi and pack of smokes waiting on the table.

In the early years, it was Walter who needed AA sponsors and they were always there for him, even in the middle of the night. He looked forward to someday repaying his debt to them. It took Walter five years or so to build enough confidence to try mentoring. In those five years Walter not only quit drinking, he also stopped smoking. Once clean of alcohol and nicotine, he stood ready and able to give back. Walter admitted that without AA he would not have survived. During the final twenty-five years of his life, Walter consistently joined AA meetings two to three days a week and freely shared his story, trying to motivate even the most downtrodden to rise up. At home, Walter proudly displayed his AA anniversary pins.

Eventually, Walter became a sponsor to hundreds of young men and women in the Greater Portland area. He also started the alcohol recovery program at the Maine Correctional Center in Windham. Walter had a lot to give, but those outside AA rarely saw it because he was modest, even hesitant and insecure, thinking, "What insight can a bum like me give to anyone?"

Few outside of AA appreciated that he was actually saving lives; getting him to share his experiences helping winos, alcoholics, and drug addicts was like pulling teeth. You really had to dig.

He was a rare creature. Realistically most of the bums who sank to Walter's depths, and stayed there for as long as he did, never got free from booze or drugs or whatever vice was ailing them. Walter, with Ann's support, was able and wanted to give back. Having been a drunk forever, he understood that world and the challenges to sobriety. He was comfortable and confident there. I met some of the men my father befriended in AA, and the tales they told about him were inspiring.

To understand my father. I sought some of them out.

I told a story earlier that when I was a teenager, a family friend was stabbed on the corner of Kellogg Street. He survived the stabbing, but continued to drink and do drugs. He was addicted to both, as well as gambling. He was in deep depression and unable to get clean when he heard my father speak at an AA meeting. He was blown away. He'd heard the wild stories about Mr. Crockett while growing up, but he had never met him. Until that meeting, he had no idea Walter was still alive, never mind sober. Walter's story moved him to clean up his act, and amazingly he did. The man is a recovering alcoholic with a loving wife, beautiful children, and a clean life. He credits Walter for being among those who saved him.

Another man, who is about my age, was even more direct.

"Your dad said 'hello' my first night in AA, but I totally blew him off. But he was persistent and he kept checking in. It took me years and too many relapses to count before I finally listened. Walter believed in me when everyone else had given up. He is my mentor, my liberator, my friend. Your father would joke, 'If I found sobriety after seventeen years on the streets and five Last Rites, you can too.' I wasn't so sure, but I trusted him, and I followed his lead. Your father saved my life."

My father was always a charmer and that came through in those AA meetings. My father also believed in second chances. He longed for forgiveness, no matter the flaws or the wounds. That was his greatest lesson to me. Once I learned it, I better understood him. And most importantly, once those walls came down after nearly fifty years, I finally gained a dad. And I finally became his son.

Chapter Twenty-Three
Being Somebody

Walter lived a sober life after he left Togus in the 1980s, but he could never escape all of his demons or entirely let go of his past. I heard rumors of brief relapses, but they were never confirmed. And if he did slip, Ann always pulled him back. Except, even Ann couldn't prevent every misstep.

On the morning of July 31, 2010, my birthday, a broker friend offered me two tickets behind home plate for that evening's Red Sox game at Fenway Park. It was around eleven o'clock when I called my father to see if he could go. I knew he would jump at the opportunity to sit five rows behind home plate to watch his beloved Red Sox. But when I called, he started waffling about going to the game. The phone conversation was strange. Walter seemed disappointed when he picked up the telephone and realized it was me.

"Hey, Dad, I just landed two tickets behind home plate at the Sox game tonight, I'll pick you up around four o'clock."

He hesitated.

"Umm, I'm not sure. I need to speak to Ann. No, sorry, I'll have to pass, I need to reach Ann."

"Is everything OK?"

"Yeah, got to go."

"OK, next time."

Hanging up the phone I knew something was off, but I didn't dwell on it. Seth was home for the summer, so the two of us went to the game instead. I felt it was odd that my father didn't call back to ask about the game, or maybe to explain why he was so rushed and needed Ann so desperately that morning.

A few weeks later in late August, I picked up a copy of *The Forecaster*. The newspaper focuses on all things local, primarily high school sports and human interest stories. However, one interesting feature is the Portland Police arrest log. Every week all arrests were listed. I read it religiously and would feign shock if somebody from my past was listed. I always knew somebody.

This week, good ol' Dad made the weekly police log. I knew that my father would barter with hookers during his drinking days. Apparently, he never got it fully out of his system. On July 31, he got pinched for soliciting a female undercover police officer for sex in downtown Portland. I took note of the date and time of the arrest. It was ten in the morning, only an hour or so before I called him about the Sox game. I just shook my head. "Will this guy always be a disappointment and embarrassment to me? Thank God Ma isn't around to see this."

I am not proud of my reaction. It had been a long time between public humiliations for my dad, and I should have been more sympathetic. After all, he had built up enough goodwill. His urgency to reach Ann was understandable. He had fucked up again and needed to explain it, maybe somehow make it right. Although I didn't see eye to eye with Ann and her relationship was frosty with my family, I had the utmost respect for her. I always wondered why she supported my father so unconditionally. She saved him, and clearly he did not make it easy. My assumption, fair or not, was that this was not his first transgression. He just got caught and had to fess up. I never mentioned the incident to them, and we never discussed it.

By the holiday season of 2010, Walter, now retired, was slowing down. He was out of his arrest funk and back to his cheerful self. Teddy, now in seventh grade, landed the Sky Masterson role in his middle school production of *Guys and Dolls.* By this point Teddy was receiving major kudos for his thespian talents. Since third grade he had been active in theater and thrived. That year he played Simon Cowell, with a British accent, in a parody of "American Idol." He followed that up with the lead in *Teddywood,* a play written for him by his music teacher that stretched from the rock 'n' roll era to current day. In sixth grade he was Lumiere, the candelabra, in *Beauty and the Beast.*

Although Walter's health forced him to miss Teddy's cross-country meets and hockey games, he still made every acting and singing performance. He wrote the *Guys and Dolls* play dates on his calendar the second I phoned him. Teddy could make his grandfather weak in the knees. Not only did Teddy have a deep voice like Walter, but my father proudly proclaimed, "It's like looking in a mirror."

Teddy was built like a young Walter, short and rugged, a very believable street thug. Walter noted, "I have to take all of this in. I love this and want to lock it into my head forever. Your boys and this role makes me feel young again." Teddy's rendition of "Luck Be a Lady" went, dare I say, even more to Walter's core than Seth's. Walter chuckled at the exaggerated dice props. By the final chorus he was bawling; just sitting in the theater with tears running down his face.

My father's life on the streets was finally catching up to him. He had recently retired from his custodian job because he just couldn't do the work any longer. He got short of breath easily and needed to rest. Retirement was relaxing, but I think inactivity hastened his decline. Although Teddy energized him, Dad wasn't getting out as much. Walter and Ann stopped at our house on Christmas Eve to exchange gifts and see the kids. Both Seth and Mattie were home from Syracuse for semester break.

It was fabulous and emotional. I'm sure my father knew his time was short, and that this might be the last time the band would be together. Seth was leaving in January to spend the spring semester in Los Angeles. My father's voice was weakening, and I think he sensed this would be their swan song. Walter soared through his repertoire of personal favorites that afternoon and early evening. Even the girls joined in, and it took all I had not to cry. It's been established that I can't sing. Ever since I got cut from the school choir in grade school, I decided not to hurt anybody's ears with my voice. I sat back, watching the concert in my living room, and felt fulfilled.

It is a wonder that my father outlived all his siblings, and his first wife, my mom. If life was predictable, this span would not be surprising—Walter was the second youngest in his family, and ten years Ma's junior. Yet, considering the life he lived, it was nothing short of a miracle that he outlived them all. Walter was a tough son of a gun. His grit was never more evident than in late 2011 when his days began to get rough, but he wouldn't give in. He just kept fighting, getting up, trying to live. It wasn't until the summer of 2012, that I noticed the twinkle in his eyes beginning to fade. He was really dying, and we couldn't do anything about it.

The man who looked death in the face five times before and said "Hell no!" was fighting his final round.

We ate lunch weekly. It was hard. Usually, he was energized and engaged in our conversations, and most of my visit was spent eating and listening. But during these lunches he could barely speak. Dementia was taking its toll. Getting anything out of him was a grind, and what did emerge came out unwillingly. He was tired and distant. Time was running out, but selfishly I wanted to see one last smile come to his face, somehow. Simply talking about the grandkids usually worked, but now he needed more. It was summer, Seth was back home and he joined us for lunch.

Seth had graduated from Syracuse University in May 2012 and was leaving for Los Angeles on Labor Day weekend. He was unsure what he wanted to do, but figured LA was the best place to find out. A few weeks before heading west we brought lunch to Grampy for what would be his final visit with Seth. Dad rallied. His grandson's presence certainly invigorated him. They spent nearly forty-five minutes talking about Seth's plans. Walter was more focused than I'd seen him in weeks and just as charming and encouraging as ever.

"Follow your dreams; don't be denied or derailed by naysayers," he told Seth.

Walter never touched his sandwich. This was now the norm. He pretty much stopped eating, and his weight was down to 120 pounds. When Seth and I left, Dad went straight to bed.

"How much time does he have left?" Seth asked.

"I don't really know; his will is weakening, but his heart is strong. If he continues to fight, maybe a year."

"Good," said Seth, "I'll see him when I get back."

It was a beautiful sentiment. He didn't need to hear that his grandfather's time was actually pressingly short. Seth left for

California a few weeks later, confident he'd see his grandfather again.

By October Walter was in the Intensive Care Unit at Maine Medical Center with tubes down his throat and up his nose, with multiple IVs flowing to keep him alive. He was 79 years old and had been sober for over thirty years, but his abused body was finally giving out. Family walked in and out of the room for hours chit-chatting and reminiscing. There was little acknowledgment from Walter other than his eyes occasionally blinking. His doctor told us it was just a matter of hours before he passed.

He asked us if we wanted a priest to come by and administer his Last Rites. Walter, although he stopped practicing his faith long ago, remained a proud Catholic and definitely wanted his sins absolved in hopes of a friendly reception at the Pearly Gates. On October 19, 2012, a priest stood over his dying body for the sixth and final time.

I got to the hospital around noon. Ann had called saying that I should come right away. I raced out of my office, leaving my coat behind, sporting a blue oxford and red striped tie, with keys and wallet in hand. My gut told me this was it.

In the hospital room with Ann and two of my Campbell cousins, I slid over next to my father's head and began rambling on about the Red Sox and anything else I thought might resonate. I hoped to see a sign that my words were getting through. I got nothing until I started chattering about his grandchildren. As I told him about Seth's adventures in Hollywood, his eyes opened wide and he nodded.

The room gasped. Everyone looked at Walter in shock. Over the next minute as I shared details of Seth's music and acting prospects, huge tears welled up in my father's eyes. He blinked and the tears ran down his cheeks. It was the first signs of life from him in more than two hours. They would be his last.

Walter fought through the evening before quietly passing in the middle of the night with his savior, Ann, by his side. My father went the distance, at long last drifting head down to his corner, before finally fading away. None of us beat death, but there was no way my dad wouldn't answer the bell. In his case he just ran out of rounds.

Walter loved many things in life, but the constants were sports, song, and suds. He took pride in supporting his grandchildren's activities. I believe in his grandsons, he saw what he wanted to be. They fulfilled his dreams as a boy and young man. Hearing their hopes restored his own.

From his earlier days, Walter yearned to be "A Somebody." He wanted to accomplish something grand and be remembered. He was a dying man who believed he had failed. Alcohol dashed the dreams of his youth and his thoughts of basking in the bright lights of success and glory. But sobriety let him live long enough to see his offspring chase such dreams. Ultimately, his legacy would not simply be as a man who became "the biggest drunk in Portland."

Seth was on set when he returned my phone call. Seth, more than anyone, understood Grampy's dreams and his desire to become "A Sombody." Once Seth learned his grandfather's death was imminent, he choked up and asked me to give my father one final message.

"Dad, tell Grampy he made it."

Epilogue

My father, Walter Franklin Crockett, passed away on October 20, 2012. That first line of his obituary in the *Portland Press Herald*—"Walter Crockett was the biggest drunk in Portland"—was true. He was the biggest drunk in town, and that's all most people knew of him. They didn't know that at the time of his death my dad had been sober for more than thirty years or that he had saved lives through Alcoholics Anonymous.

Regrettably, most readers never got beyond that first line. I received numerous calls from friends and family to see if I was upset about the article. I wasn't, only because I knew the full story, but understood and appreciated their concern. However, I couldn't shake the thought that his true legacy was overshadowed by the shocking headline.

About a year later I was hanging out with my son, Ted, in our family room and we began reminiscing about Grampy. My dad, my kids, and I frequently joked that nobody would believe his story—living on the streets for so long and receiving Last Rites five times while there—unless it was on the big screen. We were both getting emotional when Ted said, "Dad, it will never happen unless you do it."

It was the wisdom of a teenager that motivated me to tell the full story. It began with an attempt to write a screenplay, since that is what we always joked about. I quickly realized that I had no idea what I was doing and decided to just write down my thoughts. Twenty-thousand words later I had something resembling this book.

Although I didn't expect it, researching and writing this memoir proved to be cathartic. I learned a ton. About my father, my mom, and most surprisingly, myself. With my father, hope was always fleeting. It just felt like a pipe dream. But in his recovery, I started to believe

This is Martha, Seth, Ted, Mattie, and me at Acadia National Park in 2004.

again. Perhaps his greatest gift was guiding me toward forgiveness. I was hard. I'd lost faith in him and had totally written him off. Then, out of nowhere he jumps back into my life and proves me wrong. He softened me and lifted the heavy burdens that I'd been carrying since I was a child. What a relief!

I wrote this book for my children, not foreseeing it might resonate beyond family. I have always questioned what good are lessons learned if you don't pass them on. We all have struggles in life, and I respect those who prefer to keep personal information private, but concluded there isn't a right or wrong way. In this case, if our story gives even one person hope, helps them feel better about themselves or their circumstances, then sharing was the right thing to do.

In preparation for the release of this book the photo below was captured at the entrance of my childhood home. The Mayberry – Paul

– Crockett name plate lives on at 60 Kellogg Street. Considering all the change that has occurred on Munjoy Hill, seeing that nameplate brought tears to my eyes. For nearly sixty years, through multiple ownership changes, the memory of our family had stood the test of time.

The twenty-first century Munjoy Hill is nothing like the one I grew up on. Honestly, it's confounding how much has changed, and in only a half-century. In many ways it is unrecognizable to me. I often wax nostalgic driving through the old neighborhood and grudgingly accept what many others call progress. In 1970 there were six elementary and/or junior high public and parochial schools serving kids who lived on The Hill (Cathedral, Emerson, Jack, Marada Adams, North, and Shailer). Forty years later, all of those schools are closed. Jack Junior High was replaced by East End Elementary, now the one and only school on Munjoy Hill.

My first impression is always, where are all the kids? I miss the open streets with hundreds of kids running around bringing smiles to moms, dads, aunts, uncles, and grandparents all watching from their porch or stoop. Sadly, those sights and sounds have all but disappeared on The Hill, along with most of the baby boomers who

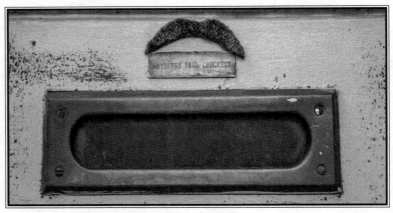

The nameplate at 60 Kellogg Street.

This is Martha and me in 2019.

grew up there. Now Munjoy Hill more closely resembles Beacon
Hill with its fine restaurants, specialty shops, and million-dollar
properties, not the rough-and-ready family hoods of yesteryear. It
remains a beautiful neighborhood, just different from what we older
Hill boys and girls remember.

Portland itself has changed dramatically since my youth. In
2018 Portland was named the No. 1 restaurant city in America by
Bon Appétit. My hometown is a foodie and craft beer destination for
tourists worldwide. As a result, property values skyrocketed, altering
the landscape and demographics permanently. In just thirty short
years, Munjoy Hill became perhaps the most desirable place to live
in Portland. How times have changed.

If nothing else, I hope it is obvious in this book that I love my
family and am proud of them. Ma's legacy is her children. She hoped

and prayed that we would grow to be positive contributors to our communities. Thanks to her and her parents: Mission accomplished. My four eldest siblings are enjoying well-earned retirements. David had a long career with Ma Bell, serving twenty years as union steward, president, and business agent. Marie had a distinguished career in the insurance industry. Jimmy was a lifelong educator. And Gin supported her husband, Bruce, and the Micucci Wholesale Grocers family.

Danny, also a lifelong educator, still teaches and coaches at Falmouth High School and is a member of the Maine Running Hall of Fame. Walt continues to thrive in the human resource industry. And Carolyn, the lone attorney in the group, is currently doing policy work for the state of Maine.

My children are all adults now. Seth teaches middle school and coaches track and cross-country. He continues to entertain us regularly in community theater. Some recent roles include Sebastian the Crab in *The Little Mermaid*, Seymour in *Little Shop of Horrors*, and the wedding singer in *The Wedding Singer*. Mattie got married two years ago, lives in Massachusetts, and works in marketing for a healthcare company. She is working toward a master's degree in global health management. Ted graduated from my alma mater, the University of Maine at Orono, in 2020 and immediately inspired us all by taking a temp job doing COVID-19 screening. Recently, Martin's Point Health Care in Portland brought him on full-time. His first move was to move out of his parents' house, making us officially empty-nesters. Martha and I are very proud.

As for Martha, she is in her twenty-first year as an education technician at Lyseth Elementary School in Portland. She is indispensable and loves her Lyseth family. I've been busy and been blessed to run Capt'n Eli's Soda for the last decade. It is the finest soda in the land. I'm also currently serving in the Maine Legislature, working hard for my neighbors. And I wrote a book.

In closing, maybe the biggest surprise of this project was the realization that my father and I were very much alike. Ironically, the man I despised and wanted nothing to do with for so long is kind of my spitting image. For the longest time I didn't want to understand my father's world or his problems. I just wanted them to go away. Our relationship certainly had its ups and downs, but I treasure every high and low. I was fortunate to have those final years with him, and appreciative I didn't waste them.

I learned during his thirty-plus years of sobriety how much we had in common. For starters, I look like my father. In sobriety there was no denying it. My dad was a humble man, both proud and modest. I try to emulate those characteristics that he exhibited while dealing with his demons in a society too quick to judge. We love sports and share the same heroes, from Carl Yastrzemski to Muhammad Ali. We even liked some of the same foods. We were meat-and-potato guys, arguably eating too many cheeseburgers and fries along the way. Ketchup was our favorite condiment, the more the better, and it went on everything. We devoured ice cream in every form.

However, it was the Italian sandwich that linked us as two odd ducks. Our order was always the same—large sandwich with no onions and ample salt, pepper, and oil. When by myself, I eat my Italian sandwich one vegetable at a time until all that remains is the ham, cheese, and roll. Then I sop up the oil and juices with the bread and eat each side of the sub individually, one then the other.

Strangely, Walter Crockett did the exact same thing.

Still today, every time I order an Italian, I think of my father. I grab my Italian, look up and say, no longer in anger, but in genuine appreciation:

"Thanks, Dad."

My siblings in 2010, clockwise from top left: Danny, Gin, Jimmy, Marie, David, Walt, Carolyn, and me.

Acknowledgments

My father's sobriety paved the way for meaningful relationships with his family. We have Ann to thank for bringing him back to us. Sadly, we lost Ann within six months of Walter's death. Some suggested that her passing was from a broken heart. For all she did for my father, and what she gave to his children and grandchildren, we are forever grateful.

This memoir would never have materialized without the support and encouragement of my siblings. You were always there for me and define what it means to be a role model. David E. Paul, Marie A. (Paul) Elder, James G. Paul, Virginia M. (Paul) Micucci, Daniel M. Paul, Walter E. Crockett, and Carolyn J. (Crockett) Russo: thank you for guiding your baby brother.

To the handful of friends who read the first draft and urged me to share our story.

To Clarke Canfield, a long-time friend and author, who read the draft and forwarded it to his editor.

To Dean Lunt, that editor, who believed in the story and its themes and brought this project to fruition.

To his team at Islandport Press. Thanks for holding my hands along the way.

To my brother Jimmy for editing the original manuscript.

To my children, Seth, Mattie, and Ted for inspiring me every single day.

To my wife Martha who supported me on this journey, "Thanks my love, for being there and doing it all."

And finally (she gets the last word), to Ma.

About the Author

Ed Crockett is a Portland businessman who is now the president of Capt'n Eli's Soda and a state representative. He was born and raised in the Munjoy Hill neighborhood of Portland, the youngest of eight children. He was raised in poverty by his mother. His father spent most of Ed's youth as a homeless alcoholic living on the streets of Portland. Ed, a graduate of Portland High School, studied broadcast journalism and earned his bachelor's degree from the University of Maine at Orono. After working for a year at WABI television in Bangor, he returned to school and earned his MBA from Boston College. Following graduate school, Ed worked for a few years in Massachusetts, Texas, and New Jersey before returning to his home state to work for some of Maine's most iconic brands, including Oakhurst Dairy, Hannaford Bros. Co., and Lepage Bakeries.

He is married to his college sweetheart, Martha Rand, and they have three children, Seth, Mattie, and Ted. Ed and Martha still live in Portland. The Ghosts of Walter Crockett is his first book.

Photo by Dave Dostie.